Antitrust
Penalty

An
Economic
Analysis

Reform

William Breit
and
Kenneth G. Elzinga

American Enterprise Institute for Public Policy Research
Washington, D.C.

William Breit is the E. M. Stevens Distinguished Professor of Economics at Trinity University in San Antonio, Texas. Kenneth G. Elzinga is a professor of economics at the University of Virginia.

Library of Congress Cataloging-in-Publication Data

Breit, William.
  Antitrust penalty reform.

  (AEI studies; 441)
  Bibliography: p.
  1. Antitrust law—United States. 2. Damages—United
States. 3. Antitrust law—Economic aspects—United
States. I. Elzinga, Kenneth G. II. Title.
III. Series.
KF1657.T7B74 1986   343.73'072'0269   86-3203
                       347.303720269
ISBN 0-8447-3600-7 (alk. paper)

1 3 5 7 9 10 8 6 4 2

AEI Studies 441

Printed in the United States of America

Contents

6   OTHER PENALTIES: INCARCERATION AND FINES   51

7   CONCLUSION   61

APPENDIX   63

NOTES TO TEXT   69

Foreword

In recent years antitrust penalty reform has become one of the main priorities of antitrust enforcement. The need for such reform has been recognized by Congress, by the courts, and by the enforcement agencies. As a result, the antitrust penalties and remedies, and in particular the treble damages provision in private suits, have come under greater scrutiny than at any other time since the passage of the Sherman Antitrust Act in 1890. This study reviews and synthesizes the recent results of research and analysis on the subject of antitrust penalty reform.

Until the early 1970s the treble damages provision of the federal antitrust laws was held to be almost sacrosanct among scholars and practitioners in the antitrust area. Most antitrust criticism was directed at the particular business practices encompassed by the laws or at the merits of a particular court decision. Complaints about antitrust penalties were almost always directed at their ineffectiveness, stemming from the inadequacy of the fines imposed on violators, the paucity of prison sentences, and the lack of structural relief. There was little if any discussion of the efficacy of the treble damages multiple or of private enforcement in general.

This situation changed after the publication of an article in the *Harvard Law Review* by William Breit and Kenneth G. Elzinga in 1973. The authors raised the question of the deterrent value of the penalties for statutory violations by examining mechanisms used to deter antitrust violations. In attempting to arrive at an optimal antitrust policy, they pointed to the critical importance of analyzing the risk attitudes of management, and they urged the replacement of the current arsenal of antitrust weapons with the unitary device of a fine based upon a percentage of corporate profits.

A year later, in an article in the *Journal of Law & Economics*, the same authors for the first time in antitrust literature subjected the treble damages provision of the laws to close scrutiny under economic theory and demonstrated its many weaknesses. In 1976, with the publication of their book, *The Antitrust Penalties: A Study in Law and Economics*, the authors carried their analysis further to examine the entire panoply of the antitrust tool kit: treble damages, fines, incarceration and dissolution, divorcement, and divestiture. They argued that in their present form the antitrust penalties were fraught with serious flaws.

Because of these efforts, a number of other scholars turned their attention to the antitrust penalties. As the academic debate intensified, the echoes eventually permeated the halls of Congress, the enforcement agencies, and the courts. It was not long before many groups outside academe called for new legislation to alter the private treble damages provision of antitrust along with the other reforms in antitrust enforcement. And this interest continues. An administrative working group has developed a variety of antitrust legislative reform proposals, with special attention to treble damages in private suits. The working group submitted recommendations for cabinet-level consideration to the Economic Domestic and Policy Councils. A package of reforms of the antitrust penalties is likely to be proposed soon for congressional action.

As a result of this reconsideration of the weaponry of antitrust, it seemed appropriate for AEI to invite William Breit and Kenneth G. Elzinga to bring their earlier work on the antitrust penalties up to date and to take a fresh look at antitrust enforcement policy. They have done so in this study by examining the public penalties of incarceration and fines and the private penalty of treble damages. Once again, their approach has been that of law and economics. The question of deterrence versus compensation as a rationale for treble damages is reopened, and the most current research on this subject is described.

One of the more recent controversial issues in antitrust, that of contribution, is also scrutinized in the light of economic theory of attitudes toward risk of corporate management. Recent research on the efficacy of jailing corporate offenders is evaluated, as are the history and consequences of imposing monetary exactions on antitrust offenders. Recent evidence on the economic costs and benefits of private actions is summarized, and current trends in antitrust penalty reform are described. Not surprisingly, Breit and Elzinga do not hesitate to present their own point of view on each issue. The result is a thoroughgoing analysis of the crucial issues surrounding antitrust penalty reform, which is now the subject of controversy and debate at the highest levels of government.

WILLIAM J. BAROODY
President
American Enterprise Institute

1
Introduction

Since its passage in 1890, the bulk of the scholarly literature and commentary on the Sherman Act has concerned its enforcement. In scores of books and articles, the question addressed has been: What kinds of economic behavior and market structures are appropriate candidates for antitrust activity? In the mainstream of antitrust writings, the debate has been over how to determine whether a particular business practice was anticompetitive. There was little discussion about what to do when it was determined to be anticompetitive. The answer seemed straightforward: use the antitrust penalties to remedy the situation, or stamp out the practice.

If the consequences of the penalties being imposed on Sherman Act violators were mentioned, the conventional wisdom was that the levy was both too small for penalizing the defendant and too inconsequential for deterring others. But careful analyses of the merits and effects of the antitrust arsenal were unusual. There was little concern, either theoretical or empirical, with antitrust's remedies and penalties.

In recent years, interest in the penalty component of antitrust laws has become more pronounced. With the increasing focus on the economic analysis of antitrust came the realization that optimal antitrust enforcement policy depended as much upon the restoration of competitive conditions as upon optimal case selection. Unless a Sherman Act violation is efficiently remedied or deterred, antitrust has secured a Pyrrhic victory.

This monograph reviews and synthesizes some of the new learning on the antitrust penalties.[1] The focus is on the "public" penalties of incarceration and fines that may be imposed following successful prosecution of government criminal cases; and on the "private" penalty of treble damages that may be levied on defendants following successful litigation brought by private parties. The approach taken here is one of law and economics, that is, endeavoring to assess the legal phenomenon of antitrust penalties from the framework of economic theory. Like most of the literature in this genre, it does not hesitate to prescribe solutions on the basis of cost-benefit analysis.

Chapter 2 examines the two rationales for treble damages actions, deterrence and compensation, and describes the new learning on these topics. Chapter 3 explores one of the most controversial issues in private enforcement, that of contribution. Chapter 4 describes the economic costs of private treble damages suits and summarizes recent evidence on them. The topic of chapter 5 is the reform, both procedural and substantive, of private actions. Chapter 6 examines other penalties for antitrust violations, tracing the current trends in the use of incarceration for Sherman Act offenders and evaluating them from the perspective of the new learning. It goes on to trace the history and consequences of imposing monetary fines on antitrust violators. Chapter 7 summarizes our conclusions.

2
The Purposes of Private Treble Damages Suits: Deterrence and Compensation

Until recently, the merits of the treble damages private action provision of the federal antitrust arsenal went almost unchallenged. There were early critics, Thurman Arnold being the most distinguished, but they were few. The literature and commentary of antitrust from the 1940s through the 1960s contained numerous criticisms of the state of antitrust, but virtually all of this literature was directed either to the merits of a particular case or a particular business practice. The authors who did discuss penalties complained about the low fines, the infrequency of imprisonment, and the lack of dissolution, divorcement, and divestiture. That the treble damages multiple needed changing (up or down), or that private enforcement itself might have drawbacks, was rarely discussed.

Beginning in the 1970s, the assessment of private treble damages actions underwent a notable change. From the scholarly literature analyzing antitrust to congressional debates on the subject, the interest in penalties and remedies has grown. Moreover, the tenor of this literature with regard to treble damages actions has been almost uniformly critical.

This critical literature's diversity is as notable as its growth. More than one commentator has alleged that antitrust can be divided into two major camps.[2] Presumably each camp holds positions that differ on enough issues to warrant the taxonomy of opposing camps. Nonetheless, with regard to private treble damages enforcement of the antitrust laws, there has been sharp criticism from each camp.

Representing the University of Chicago position, Richard Posner has written that the "burgeoning of the private antitrust action has induced enormous, and I think justified, concern about the overexpansion of the antitrust laws and their increasing use to retard rather than promote competition."[3] Michael Spence of Harvard University was quoted recently as saying that with the Antitrust Division's enforcement, "you generally end up with sensible decisions. But official policy is not the whole story. I worry more about private antitrust—people suing other people under the antitrust laws. Things can get carried away, and antitrust law can be used in ways that are not desirable. . . ."[4] From the *Journal of Law & Economics*, the unofficial organ of the Chicago school of antitrust, came the initial attack on private antitrust enforcement.[5] In the Areeda and Turner treatise, the unofficial bible of the Harvard approach, one also finds the enthusiasm for private enforcement under tight rein.[6]

Buttressed by this literature, numerous groups outside the academy have called for legislation altering the private treble damages method of antitrust enforcement. Senator Strom Thurmond, chairman of the Senate Committee on the Judiciary, has indicated his committee "may well want to face the question of whether certain antitrust violations warrant single rather than treble private damages."[7] Congressman Peter W. Rodino, chairman of the House Committee on the Judiciary, has asserted that "the issue of treble damages is ripe for hearings"[8] and recently commissioned a study of private antitrust actions and the contemporary assault upon them.[9]

In an earlier time, scholars debated whether the purpose of private antitrust enforcement was to deter antitrust violations or to compensate those injured by them.[10] While this particular debate never caught the public's fancy, the question is not unimportant. If the purpose of section 4 of the Clayton Act is to compensate those who have been injured by antitrust violations, then the research agenda for scholars is quite different than if the goal is deterrence. In the language of public finance, compensation is at root a question pertaining to incidence. Deterrence, on the other hand, is at root a question pertaining to the decision calculus of the entrepreneur.

If, for example, compensation for society's loss were the sole objective of private antitrust enforcement, a mechanical application of Marshallian economics would require convicted members of a cartel to make reparations in an amount equivalent to the deadweight loss it imposed upon its customers (and presumably some of its noncustomers, that is, individuals who were priced out of the market by the cartel price). If deterrence were the goal, a payment equated with deadweight loss would be too small, even in a world with costless certainty of detection and conviction and no uncertainty as to what the law proscribed. The deadweight loss may be smaller than the expected monopoly profits gained from the cartel's collective output restriction; consequently, the cartel would go undeterred.[11] Estimating the payment needed for deterrence requires an understanding of

4

all the risk-adjusted costs and benefits of an illegal action that has an uncertain chance of detection and conviction.

In the next two sections on the purpose of private antitrust enforcement, we follow this distinction. The first section describes the new learning on private actions from the standpoint of optimal deterrence, ignoring the locus and magnitude of injury. The second section examines the goal of compensation and considers the new learning on optimal deterrence under a compensatory framework.

The New Learning on Deterrence

Four propositions about deterrence make up the new learning.

1. The optimal sanction depends on both the attitudes of corporate managers toward risk and the probability of their apprehension and conviction for antitrust violations.

2. Efficient enforcement does not imply deterrence of all antitrust violations when there are enforcement costs.

3. Even if enforcement costs are zero, optimal deterrence would not mean 100 percent deterrence because, in some instances, the gain to the wrongdoer or to society will be greater than the harm to the victim.

4. There is a significant difference between deterring antitrust violations privately through the enticement of collecting damages and enforcing those prohibitions publicly through fines without compensation (since a system of deterrence relying on compensation as the spur to enforcement changes the incentives of those potentially compensated, thereby potentially generating unintended and adverse side effects).

These propositions underlie most recent discussions of the deterrence issue by economists and economically oriented legal scholars.

Risks and Probabilities. The first proposition is the extension to antitrust of Gary Becker's profound treatment of the deterrence of criminal activity.[12] Becker was the first modern economist to apply economic theory to illegal activities in a formal manner. He introduced the notion of attitudes toward risk as a key element in devising an optimal system of sanctions for unlawful behavior.

Becker integrated the economics of criminal behavior into the general framework of the theory of choice. He treated the decision to engage in criminal activity as a calculated act in which the potential offender compares the expected utility from the offense with the utility derived from using his resources elsewhere. Becker postulated a function relating the number of offenses committed by any person to his probability of conviction and to his punishment. He then showed that an increase in one of the variables compensated by an equal percentage reduction in the other variable would not change the expected income from an offense but, because the amount of risk would change, it would alter the expected utility depending upon the attitude toward risk.

In addition, Becker made a strong case for fines instead of other punishments as the rationale for the criminal code. Because all punishments can be reduced to their monetary equivalent, and fines do not consume resources (as imprisonment does), fines equal to the harm inflicted on society by the illegal behavior would be the optimal sanction. The argument is made very general and powerful by stressing the minimization of the social loss. Fines have the virtue of deterring by simply transferring wealth without reducing social wealth or income. Imprisonment reduces the wealth or income of the malefactor with no compensating offset. It does this at a cost to others as well as to the criminal. The chief conclusion of his paper was that optimal policies to combat illegal behavior are part of a system for allocating resources optimally.

This contribution resurrected and improved the work of Cesare Beccaria and Jeremy Bentham, who applied an economic calculus to crime, an approach that went out of favor one hundred years before Becker. Becker's article was a breakthrough and turned the attention of many economists to an economic framework for studying illegal activity. It was only a matter of time before antitrust would be analyzed using the Becker model.

Attitudes toward risk must be taken into account to determine the proper penalty structure for antitrust violations. If potential cartelists were risk preferrers, the penalty for violating the antitrust laws would have more deterrent effect if the probability of apprehension and conviction were large and the actual damages to be paid in the event of conviction were low. This is true because a risk preferrer would receive greater expected utility from the small probability of a large loss than from the large probability of a small loss. So in devising an efficient deterrent mechanism, his preferences in that regard should be taken into consideration. Since he would prefer the small probability of a large loss, our laws should be designed to make him face a large probability of a small loss. Enforcing such laws would involve greater resources devoted to apprehension and conviction of violators with a "compensating" reduction in the amount of the penalty, either in the form of fines or damages.

If the potential cartelist were risk averse, the opposite policy would be called for. Since a risk-averse individual prefers—receives greater utility from—the large probability of a small loss to the small probability of a large loss, the optimal enforcement mechanism would attempt to thwart him in the enjoyment of ill-gotten gains. Instead he would face a high monetary exaction combined with a lower probability of detection and conviction. His demand for cartelization would therefore fall relative to his choice under the opposite trade-offs. If managers were risk neutral, risk attitudes would not have to be taken into account in devising the most efficient sanction. The potential wrongdoer would be concerned only with the expected value of his gains and not with their expected utility.

Considerations such as these led Breit and Elzinga to propose the use of a high fine with a lower probability of detection as the most efficient deterrent of antitrust violations.[13] The proposal was based on the perception that modern corporate management is risk averse and that private suits have adverse side effects that make them inefficient compared with the public action alternative, which requires no compensation. Deterrence, not compensation, is stressed as the goal of the antitrust laws.[14]

A. Mitchell Polinsky and Steven Shavell raise the possibility that the proposal of a high fine and a small probability of detection is not optimal if the increased risk imposed by the high fine imposes an additional disutility on persons subject to the fine that exceeds the additional utility from spending less on enforcement.[15] This would occur if there are errors in attributing price-fixing to firms or if the cartel agreement generates gains in society's wealth that compensate for the loss from collusive price fixing.[16] Warren Schwartz, however, has made the offsetting observation that in the case of risk aversion a high fine combined with a small probability of apprehension might be optimal because of the incentive it would provide innocent defendants to spend an amount in litigation that might greatly reduce the error rate in antitrust enforcement.[17]

One of the surprising results of Becker's work on the application of risk attitudes to the deterrence of illegal activity is the insight that the fine imposed need not equal the social cost of the crime. It is only the *expected* value of the fine that should equal social cost.[18] If the probability of imposing the fine is less than one, then, in order to make the expected punishment cost equal to the social cost, the fine must be greater than the social cost of the illegal activity. As the probability of apprehension and conviction falls, the fine increases to compensate for the fall in the expected cost of punishment. This is the justification for the use of multiple damages rather than single damages as a deterrent. Any optimal antitrust sanction must take probabilities as well as risk attitudes into account.[19]

Deterrence with Enforcement Costs. The second proposition of the new learning regarding deterrence—that efficient enforcement does not imply complete deterrence of all antitrust violations when enforcement costs are positive—also followed Becker's lead. Its application to antitrust was made by Elzinga and Breit in 1976.[20] They argued that antitrust enforcement imposes significant costs on society. Resources are consumed by the federal antitrust enforcement agencies and by the administration of the courts. Also, there are costs of negotiation and litigation incurred by plaintiffs and defendants. In addition, there are resources used by other federal and state agencies affected by antitrust activity. These costs rise with increasing antitrust enforcement as increasing amounts of society's scarce resources are devoted to antitrust activities. Moreover, these costs grow more quickly at the same time that increasing antitrust enforcement provides diminishing benefits. The best results, therefore, would be achieved where the marginal social costs and benefits are equal, a position short of creating perfect competition. Only in the case where the marginal costs to society of additional antitrust enforcement were zero would perfect competition be the appropriate goal; then the achievement of perfect competition would coincide with the maximization of net benefits to society.

Since raising fines is essentially a costless procedure, it has special appeal in the antitrust arena. The proposition that the cost of antitrust enforcement makes the attainment of the conditions implied by perfect competition an inefficient policy has been named "the Elzinga-Breit theorem."[21] Li Way Lee argued that an implication of this theorem is that antitrust can be viewed as a duopoly game in which the antitrust enforcement agency faces the cartel. The optimal level of enforcement depends on the anticipated response of the cartel. The Elzinga-Breit model therefore is best understood as a Stackelberg game in which the antitrust agency is the leader and the cartel the follower. Lee demonstrated that the theorem stands up well under a Cournot-Nash behavioral assumption in which both the agency and the cartel take each other's spending level as given. Robert W. Feinberg showed that given optimal choices by the cartel, at the Cournot-Nash equilibrium, optimal enforcement is that level of effort that maximizes the net benefits of antitrust policy.[22]

The Optimal Antitrust Sanction. The third proposition of the new learning (that optimal deterrence does not imply 100 percent deterrence even if enforcement costs are zero when the gain to the wrongdoer or to society is greater than the harm to the victim) is one of the more subtle and surprising conclusions of the economic approach to

8

penalties. It introduces the notion of the "efficient offense." Once the possibility of efficient offenses is taken into account, penalties can be too high as well as too low. Thus, even if a fine is socially costless in terms of resources expended to increase its value, its increased deterrent effect could choke off socially beneficial behavior. For example, mergers might involve cost reductions greater than allocative losses caused by the combination. Frank Easterbrook uses the term "false positive" to refer to a fine or damage award that eliminates desirable price reductions resulting from actions that might be ruled "predatory" but that result in lower prices, greater output, product innovations, and the like.[23] Because false positives are possible, it is necessary to devise a sanction for antitrust violations that encourages efficient offenses and discourages inefficient ones.

The familiar demand and cost functions of figure 1 bring out the range of interpretations of an optimal fine or sanction more explicitly. Assume that a firm operating in a perfectly competitive market enters into a collusive agreement to restrict output. At competitive price P_0 the firm produces output Q_0. After engaging in a collusive agreement the firm cuts back its output to Q_1 charging a price of P_1. The loss in consumers' surplus is the trapezoid P_1DEP_0. Part of this loss represents a transfer to the cartelists, the rectangle P_1DRP_0, leaving as the net loss to society the triangle DER. At first glance, it might appear that an optimal sanction would deter all such behavior and would do so by fining the cartelist the amount of the rectangle P_1DRP_0 since that is the amount of the cartelist's gain. Thus, for example, William H. Page argues that ". . . the full overcharge [which would be the profit rectangle] is a proper measure of damages."[24] If that gain were eliminated, the incentive for collusive action on the cartelist's part would disappear.

But this is clearly wrong since the cartelist is interested not only in the value of this gain but also in its utility. The penalty would have to be adjusted for the risk attitude of the cartelist as well as for the probability of detection and conviction. If there were a one-third probability of apprehension and if the cartelist were risk neutral, the firm would be deterred by multiplying the rectangle by three: treble damages would be optimal for producing 100 percent deterrence. This solution would be incorrect, however, if the cartelist were risk averse or risk preferring, or if the probability of detection and conviction were greater or less than one-third. But even if we knew with certainty that all cartelists were risk neutral and that the precise probability of detection and conviction were equal to one, the profit rectangle P_1DRP_0 would be the incorrect measure on which to base the damage judgment. This is true because of the possibility that the cartel would

FIGURE 1

ILLUSTRATION OF WEALTH LOSSES AND TRANSFERS UNDER
CARTEL AGREEMENT

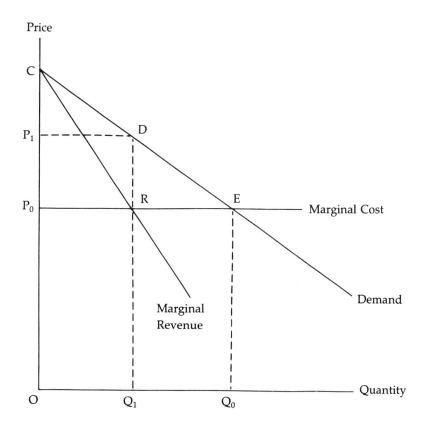

generate cost savings. That is, the agreement among the firms to collude might cause the firms to take into account technical diseconomies they impose on each other.[25] If so the firm would not be deterred from engaging in the cartel activity even when it imposes a deadweight loss on society in an amount greater than the allocative efficiencies generated by the cartel. Thus a fine in the amount of the profit rectangle P_1DRP_0 would lead to under-deterrence.

Another choice for the optimal penalty is the deadweight loss triangle DER. Warren F. Schwartz, for example, suggests that the imposition of such a fine would be optimal since it would require the offender to pay the complete social costs of his offense. If the offender pays the amount DER back to society, and that is the full amount of its inefficiency, how could there be any objection? Even if the profit rectangle P_1DRP_0 is greater than the deadweight loss DER, and the cartel continues to operate, society is recompensed for any losses imposed on it. If the profit rectangle is less than the deadweight loss, the firm will be deterred from the illegal activity.[26]

But Schwartz's rule would be incorrect if the cartelist's monopoly profits *plus* any cost savings from cartelization are greater than the deadweight loss while the cost savings alone are smaller than the deadweight loss. For in that case the cartelist would continue to engage in collusive behavior. Yet the gain to society in savings would be smaller than the deadweight loss. Once again there would be under-deterrence.

Richard Posner and Frank Easterbrook have suggested that the optimal fine would be the monopoly profit rectangle plus the deadweight loss (adjusted for the probability of detection and conviction).[27] In terms of figure 1, the sanction would be the trapezoid P_1DEP_0, that is, the total loss in consumers' surplus. It seems that all geometric bases are covered in the literature on optimal deterrence.

The trick to discovering the optimal sanction is to find a rule that will force the potential cartelist to compare any cost saving from his activity with the deadweight loss triangle. If the cost saving were larger than the deadweight loss, it would be in his (and society's) interest to undertake the illegal activity. So after he deducts the monopoly profit rectangle (which is only part of the fine to be paid under the Posner-Easterbrook rule), the cartelist will examine the deadweight loss (the remainder of the fine to be paid) and compare it with the value of the cost saving. The fine that is the sum of the deadweight triangle plus the profit rectangle is the correct sanction since it will encourage the "right" amount of illegal antitrust activity. Damages larger than this (that is, a fine larger than the area DER plus P_1DRP_0 could lead to over-deterrence, for in that case the potential offender would be comparing the wrong magnitudes. After paying the trapezoid P_1DEP_0, the remaining part of the fine to be paid would be compared with the cost saving from the illegal activity. If it is larger than that amount, the potential cartelist would be deterred from forming the cartel. But this would be incorrect from a social standpoint if the deadweight loss triangle were in fact less than the cost saving. Although he states it differently, William Landes's rule, "the optimal fine should equal the net harm to persons other than the offender"[28] is, in effect, the same as the Posner-Easterbrook optimal sanction.

Therefore, the Posner-Easterbrook penalty causes the antitrust violator to compare any efficiency gains of the violation to the deadweight loss to society. The antitrust violator must be made to forgo his monopoly overcharge (rectangle P_1DRP_0) in order to give him the proper incentives to make the correct comparison. Only a fine equal to the total loss in consumers' surplus brings about this result.

A numerical example may help to clarify the concept of the optimal antitrust sanction. Assume that a potential cartelist calculates that joining a horizontal price-fixing conspiracy will increase his profits by $100 million. He also is aware that the deadweight loss imposed on society by his activity is $50 million. If the expected value of the fine imposed is the entire amount of consumers' surplus ($150 million) would he enter the cartel? He would do so if he believed that the cartel would be accompanied by cost reductions to him greater than $50 million. If the cost saving were, say, $60 million, he would still enter the price-fixing conspiracy because he would know that his fine would be $100 million (his cartel profits) plus $50 million (the deadweight loss) leaving him $10 million more revenue than would be the case if he did not enter the cartel. In this case the cartel is accompanied by cost reductions greater than the deadweight loss it imposes on society. On efficiency grounds, it should be permitted.

The discovery of the correct rule for an optimal antitrust sanction is important since such a penalty will not deter a firm from an efficient antitrust violation. It is, as Landes put it, "a simple and, once explained, obvious rule for bringing about the efficient level of offenses."[29] As such it is one of the significant insights that make up the new learning on deterrence.

Questioning Private Actions. Although the new learning on deterrence has crystallized the optimal penalty for antitrust enforcement, there is less agreement on what institutional structure would most likely bring about the result of optimal deterrence. In the public sector the maximum fine is $1 million for corporations and $100,000 for individuals. But it is generally agreed that these figures are inadequate to bring about the right amount of deterrence.

Many private treble damages actions follow a successful federal prosecution. The private action treble damages award is the most important deterrent. There is, however, an inevitable conflict in relying on both private and public enforcement of antitrust. It would be purely coincidental if two uncoordinated enforcement institutions produced the optimal sanction.

There is no reason to believe that the present mixed system arrives at the correct solution. It has been demonstrated that private enforcement has many inefficiencies. The present treble damages approach leads to adverse side effects in the form of "perverse incentives" and "misinformation." In addition, private actions that rely on compensation to generate enforcement efforts by private aggrieved parties create reparations costs.[30]

The problem of achieving the optimal level of deterrence under the alternatives of private versus public enforcement has been the subject of much discussion. Becker and Stigler, for example, have argued that most of the adverse effects of private enforcement would be eliminated if individuals or firms that discover the violation received the fine.[31] On the other side, Landes and Posner demonstrated that relying on entrepreneurial law firms or private plaintiffs could lead to over-deterrence. The correct combinations of probabilities and fines could not be achieved in the private sector because every increase in the fine (in the form of multiplied damages) would lead to increased enforcement. Under public enforcement the fine could be raised while the probability of detection and conviction could be reduced.[32] There is no consensus and so no clear-cut new learning on the subject. What *is* new is the questioning of the private action approach, once considered sacrosanct.

Empirical Evidence. Empirical investigations into the deterrent effects of antitrust enforcement provide some clues regarding the efficacy of the present system. This research is in the earliest stages. Undoubtedly, it will be important in supplementing the simple economic models of law enforcement that have so far dominated the literature.

The pioneering study using stock market data to assess antitrust deterrence was by James Ellert.[33] For the years 1935–1971, he estimated the effect of antitrust enforcement on shareholder returns in the period before and after the litigation of antitrust complaints. His study revealed that respondents in Federal Trade Commission (FTC) cases experienced unusually high rates of return prior to the announcement of the FTC complaint. But the effect of the FTC action on shareholder wealth was insignificant. Ellert attributed this to the lack of significant penalties in the FTC's arsenal and to the agency's policy of not sharing with potential private litigants information gleaned from its investigations.

Antitrust actions by the Department of Justice, Ellert found, regularly did produce negative effects on defendant share prices, averaging about 1.6 percent of the firm's market value in the month of the indictment (an average of $7.5 million). Because these amounts substantially exceeded the dollar value of Sherman Act fines being levied at that time, Ellert argued that the losses were associated with

13

the effect of private treble damages action that could follow a successful Antitrust Division prosecution. He concluded:

> The statistical evidence of this study suggests that private damage awards can be substantial, particularly out-of-court settlements which constitute the majority of outcomes in private antitrust proceedings. Justice Department investigations reduce the costs of discovery for potential private claimants and encourage secondary private actions. Nolo pleas and charges of collusive price-fixing are likely to leave defendants most vulnerable to successful private suits. Defendants experience negative relative share price performance only during the period before the statute of limitations runs on private actions. Thereafter, normal share price behavior is observed. In actions where there is not cause for private suits (deceptive practices cases), and in actions where private plaintiffs have not recorded favourable court rulings (merger cases), we do not observe significant deterioration of shareholder wealth after the resolution of government proceedings.[34]

Malcolm R. Burns analyzed the competitive effects of the December 1911 dissolution orders carried out against Standard Oil, American Tobacco, and American Snuff.[35] He used monthly stock prices to track changes that accompanied significant developments in the litigation. Burns discovered that investors respond quickly to new information. The filing of the complaints against Standard Oil and American Tobacco, for example, reduced the value of snuff, tobacco, and petroleum securities by 9 to 16 percent, an amount that would gain the attention of management and shareholder alike. But these price declines were reversed by news of the reorganization of each firm. When these plans were published, the stock price increases canceled the initial declines. Astute traders believed the dissolution orders would have no effect on the value of discounted earnings per share.

The most important result coming out of this study, quite apart from corroborating other literature on the ineffectiveness of dissolution orders, is the conclusion, consistent with Ellert's work, that security prices are highly sensitive to new information regarding antitrust enforcement. Burns's work pointed up the importance of such data for future study of antitrust policy. Indeed five years later, Kenneth D. Garbade, William L. Silber, and Lawrence J. White made use of stock prices to study the market's response to the filing of antitrust suits using a sample of thirty-four companies named in the suits.[36] In contrast to the Burns study, which used monthly data, Garbade, Silber, and White based their analysis on daily data, allowing for a more precise estimate of the effect of antitrust filings. They concluded that, on average, the price of a stock in a company against which a suit has been filed by the Department of Justice or the Federal Trade Commission moves downward roughly 6 percent within four trading days. Using cross-sectional data, they estimated that the magnitude of the drop is related to the probable effects of the action on future earnings prospects.

Dosoung Choi and George C. Philippatos went beyond the study of market prices and tested for profitability.[37] They compared a sample of large manufacturing corporations indicted for violations of the Sherman Act between 1958 and 1972 with a matching control group of unindicted firms. The indicted firms showed decreasing profitability as a result of the antitrust case. The inference follows that an antitrust case has a deterrent effect on pricing behavior. The largest decrease in profitability, however, was experienced by first-time violators. The study also found that an antitrust case did not result in any significant changes in the firms' financial leverage or growth.

The first systematic attempt to estimate the results of antitrust enforcement on horizontal price-fixing in a specific industry was that of Michael K. Block, Frederick C. Nold, and Joseph G. Sidak.[38] They used data on the bread industry in an attempt to assess empirically the deterrent effect of private and public enforcement on the decision to engage in collusion. They assumed that the probability of being investigated for price-fixing was positively related to the markup level. One reason is that higher markups may provoke more complaints to the Department of Justice. In addition, the greater the ability of a cartel to prevent cheating by individual members (which raises markups), the greater the conspiracy's detectability. Building on this assumption, the authors concluded that antitrust penalties do not necessarily eliminate price-fixing but are likely to reduce the optimal markup. They tested the proposition that penalties against price-fixing are an effective deterrent by using the Antitrust Division's annual budget as an indirect measure of enforcement capability. The evidence suggested a deterrent effect of enforcement efforts; that is, an increase in the antitrust budget reduced markups on white bread. Moreover, the bringing of a price-fixing case itself may have consequences for undetected collusion. Their results suggested that a price-fixing case against bread bakers in one city causes lower markups by bakers in neighboring cities. They partitioned their sample into the periods before and after class actions became a credible threat in the bread industry. Since all but one of the class actions followed a Department of Justice case, they assumed that the class actions affected the penalty cost, not the probability of detection. Their estimates were consistent

15

with the hypothesis that class actions are the most effective penalty. This means that deterrence then was a function of both public and private enforcement.

More recently, Block and Nold, in collaboration with Jonathan Feinstein, have analyzed data on activity in the construction industry, particularly with regard to bid-rigging on highway construction projects.[39] With the change to a larger number of prosecutions in this industry and larger penalties assessed upon price fixers, the authors could assess the deterrence effect of the Justice Department's enforcement efforts. They found that antitrust activity reduced the amount of bid-rigging. They argue that the deterrence effect came more from the higher penalties imposed upon offenders than from the increased probability of detection and conviction, an empirical finding of particular relevance for our later discussion of the optimal mix of private and public enforcement.

Edward A. Snyder's recent contribution to this literature was to attempt to measure not only the deterrence effects of increases in antitrust penalties, but also the extent to which higher penalties induce defensive efforts by firms to avoid violations and penalties.[40] In Snyder's model of corporate behavior, firms face the binary choice between legal and illegal activity; moreover, firms operate in a world where innocent parties may be convicted. As a consequence, firms engage in activities that reduce the chance of conviction and attendant penalties, including the substitution away from legal activities due to the possibility of erroneous conviction. Snyder argued that excessive penalties may deter anticompetitive behavior but may also encourage costly defensive efforts by both offenders and nonoffenders if conviction errors are possible. Among his findings are that the congressional increases in the antitrust sanctions made in 1974 did deter antitrust violations such as price-fixing, but that the increased penalties made it more difficult to prosecute the remaining violations because of increased defensive efforts. In particular, he found that higher criminal penalties and higher treble damages penalties from subsequent private actions encouraged defendants to eschew pleading guilty.

These empirical studies are tentative steps toward measurement of the effects of antitrust enforcement. As Robert J. Reynolds has emphasized, however, none of the requisite empirical data is now available to settle such crucial questions as the right amount of enforcement, the appropriate mix between public and private enforcement, and the precise penalty for offenders.[41] He criticized the efforts that have been made to measure the effects of antitrust enforcement by the examination of individual antitrust cases, since this measurement captures only a small part of the effects produced by a case in all markets. Also he indicates that a better understanding is needed of the interaction between the enforcement strategies of the antitrust agencies and the strategic response of firms.[42]

The New Learning on Deterrence under a Compensatory Framework

Deterrence versus Compensation. Are private treble damages suits a mechanism for franchising thousands of private attorneys general for additional deterrence, or are they a compensatory mechanism for making amends to injured persons? One response to this question is to consider the language of section 4 of the Clayton Act. The statute refers to an "injury" to a plaintiff's "business or property" before multiple damages can be recovered. If statutory language alone were the basis for discerning congressional meaning on the question of deterrence versus compensation, the nod would go to compensation.

If deterrence were the sole objective, it would not matter who received the award, as long as it did not go to the violator. There would be no need for a successful plaintiff to show injury to its own business or property. Moreover, under a deterrence objective the amount of the payment is not necessarily the amount of injury. Rather it is the expected value sufficient to deter (and not so large as to over-deter) the antitrust violation. That amount could be less or greater than the trebled magnitude of injury sustained by a private plaintiff. Thus the statutory language poses an additional problem for antitrust policy: how to achieve the goal of optimal deterrence given the compensatory language of section 4.

Three Hurdles to Compensation. The litigation process for a prevailing private plaintiff is sometimes divided into three hurdles: (1) antitrust liability must be shown, that is, there must be proof of an antitrust violation; (2) the "fact of damage" must be shown, that is, there must be proof that the plaintiff has been harmed economically; and (3) the amount of damage must be shown, that is, there must be proof of the magnitude of harm—the amount to be trebled. For plaintiffs able to ride the coattails of successful government prosecution—where liability already has been shown—the number of hurdles is reduced by one.

If one borrows an analogy from personal injury litigation, the distinction between steps two and three and their ordering will seem logical. A person allegedly injured by a falling tower (to use a Biblical illustration) must prove, as step two, that the edifice landed on him.

17

The next hurdle, predicated upon the first but distinguishable from it, is to estimate the pecuniary magnitude of the harm. The distinction between the two steps, while helpful, can be overdrawn when translated into the world of antitrust. A decision as to whether a physician has been injured (step two) by exclusion from a particular hospital might be reached only through an inquiry that would ascertain the magnitude of the injury (step three).

The evolution of the legal standards of eligibility to recover damages and how the Court reached its present position is a tale worth telling, but not here. Suffice it to say that at an earlier time, both hurdles two and three were lower than they are now, which made life easier for the private litigant. One commentator concluded that these hurdles were so readily crossed that "every nominal violation that held out the prospect of treble damages would be challenged regardless of its effects on competition."[43]

The New Learning Standard. In attempting to approach the goal of optimal deterrence, one encounters the compensatory language of section 4. The statute forecloses the direct use of an optimal fine, for it requires that a plaintiff's recovery be "threefold the damages by him sustained."[44] Thus courts must formulate recovery with an eye toward compensation and not simply consider deterrence objectives. Even more problematic is the apparent breadth of the statute, for it authorizes a right to compensation through treble damages for "any person who shall be injured in his business or property by reason of anything forbidden in the antitrust laws."[45] Taken literally, this language would render the goal of optimal deterrence unattainable because of the "ripple effects" of anticompetitive behavior throughout the economy.

But courts have been willing to construe this language narrowly,[46] thereby enabling consideration of the goal of optimal deterrence within the framework of section 4. To achieve optimal deterrence under the present statutory framework, there must be some constraint upon the scope of liability for antitrust violations.[47] Only by limiting the type of injuries that are eligible for compensation can one prevent the award of treble damages in cases involving noneconomic theories of liability and bring damage awards closer to the optimal fine. To this end, the new learning indicates a profound change in antitrust doctrine, for it incorporates an efficiency criterion into the designation of who is eligible to recover treble damages.[48]

Under the new learning, a plaintiff is not permitted to be a "private attorney general" and to be compensated through treble damages for his efforts unless he has suffered "antitrust injury."[49] There must be a correlation between the injury to his "business or property" and business behavior by a defendant that the antitrust laws would want to deter because the behavior is anticonsumer. The new learning would limit the scope of private actions to those where there is a congruence between the aims of the private antitrust bar and the aims of public antitrust agencies motivated solely by economic goals of antitrust in their case selection. This approach would remove the trebling incentive that provokes lawsuits based on noneconomic theories of liability. In a nutshell, plaintiffs who perceived they had been treated "unfairly" (often distributors and competitors of a defendant firm) would not be eligible to recover under section 4 because the effect of their suits would not square with preventing output-restricting practices.[50]

In addition to limiting treble damages suits to output-restricting violations, the requirement that a plaintiff suffer antitrust injury also serves to limit damage awards associated with those violations. Because there is a risk of deterring efficient offenses, every plaintiff injured through an output-restricting violation should not be eligible for treble damages. Instead, only those plaintiffs whose injuries are caused by the anticompetitive aspect of the violation should be compensated through treble damages if there is to be a regime of compensatory damages.[51] If a merger were to lead to an output restriction, for example, causing a monopolistic overcharge to consumers, and the merger also caused productive efficiencies that reduced employment for workers, consumers would suffer antitrust injury and be eligible to recover treble damages while discharged employees would not. Thus the doctrine of antitrust injury helps "to keep damage awards related to the real social costs of violations in order to avoid overdeterrence."[52]

The new learning, then, is conceptually pristine. Only antitrust cases that would lead to expanding output could secure treble damages for private plaintiffs. One immediate advantage of such a focus is to reduce the current complexity and uncertainty regarding who may recover and to eliminate the arbitrary character of current standing rules.[53] Currently, for example, ongoing customers of a cartel may recover treble damages; noncustomers who would have bought at the competitive price may not recover, even though their loss of consumer surplus may exceed that of actual customers, and arguably they are more deserving of compensatory damages. But more to the point, the effect of this approach to antitrust injury would limit the number of private actions that could be brought. Lawsuits in which a plaintiff's theory on liability is not consistent with promoting efficiency would not proceed. For those in the "Chicago school" tradition of antitrust, this would be a laudatory limitation.

Although the requirement that a plaintiff suffer antitrust injury contributes to the attainment of optimal deterrence, it is unable to solve every problem associated with the language of the statute. In order for a damage award to bring about optimal deterrence, for example, its *expected* value must be equivalent to the optimal penalty. Thus a damage award must be adjusted upward if the probability of apprehension and conviction for a violation is less than one. Although the trebling factor of section 4 serves this function, it does so in a very crude manner. For some violations (for instance, price-fixing), the probability of apprehension and conviction may be less than one-third; consequently underdeterrence will occur. Similarly, less concealable violations are likely to hold out a probability of apprehension, and conviction of greater than one-third and will be overdeterred.

In addition to difficulties associated with mandatory trebling, optimal deterrence according to the doctrine of antitrust injury involves trade-offs. By limiting compensable harms to those that reflect the anticompetitive effect of the violation, efficient enforcers of the antitrust laws may be sacrificed. Under the doctrine of antitrust injury, for example, an employee who is fired for refusing to participate in a price-fixing scheme is unable to recover treble damages for his injuries.[54] Such an employee has unique access to information and may be an effective private attorney general. Nevertheless, given the existence of efficient offenses and the proliferating effect of many antitrust violations, if optimal deterrence is to be achieved, the universe of compensable harms must be limited. Thus by pursuing optimal deterrence, the use of potentially efficient private enforcers of the antitrust laws may be sacrificed. This paradox illustrates how difficult it is to achieve optimal deterrence within a compensatory framework. The doctrine of antitrust injury goes a long way toward achieving this goal, but it remains doubtful whether optimal deterrence can ever be fully achieved under the present statutory language.

As we discussed in the previous section, the new learning on private enforcement flies the flag of deterrence, not of compensation. A major justification for this is that optimally framed deterrence measures would practically eliminate any need for efforts at compensation. Therefore the focus of the literature has been on constructing optimal private and public exactions from antitrust violators that would deter. The problem of compensation becomes the wrong one to address. Underscoring this neglect is the belief that the task itself borders on being intractable.

A monopolist or cartelist imposes a tax of sorts upon consumers. Just as a government-imposed tax drives a wedge between the relative prices faced by the consumer and the producer in the market, so too a monopolist or cartelist, in charging a price above marginal cost, alters the proportions and relative quantities in which different consumer goods and intermediate products are produced and in which the services of factors are combined. The complexities and disagreements that exist in the scholarly literature on tax incidence parallel the problem of measuring antitrust damages. As Posner asserted:

> Everybody's economic welfare is bound up with everybody else's. Why stop with the ultimate consumer? If he is forced to pay a high price for a product, his demand for other products will fall and this may hurt the suppliers of those products, and the suppliers' suppliers, and so on ad infinitum.[55]

Nonetheless, damages *are* assessed. It is useful to inquire whether the new learning on antitrust has affected the estimation process. We show here that the new learning has had a methodological effect. Moreover, our impression is that a pronounced effect has come about through the courts' elevation of the hurdle of damages estimation.

The Assessment of Damages. For decades the doctrine prevailed that of all the hurdles in private enforcement, damage estimation was the lowest.[56] The standards of proof operated in a methodological framework in which damages estimates were to be constructed in one of two ways: (1) the amount of overcharge, for example in the case of a customer buying from a cartel and (2) the lost profits or the lower value of a business subject to a collective boycott for example.

Overcharge. The arithmetic of the overcharge concept is simple enough. After a comparison of prices before and after the antitrust violation, or through a yardstick comparison with a contemporaneous situation, a court selects a "competitive price." The court awards the plaintiff the difference between the competitive estimate and the amount paid, times the quantity purchased, trebled. The standard reference on the overcharge methodology is to the electrical equipment cases.[57] In countless private actions since this celebrated conspiracy (most of them involving negotiated settlements), economists, lawyers, and accountants have teamed up to produce charts displaying competitive prices, a divergence when the alleged anticompetitive behavior began, and a return to normal on the heels of an indictment.

Conceptually, the before-and-after approach has remained intact. *Methodologically*, however, there has been a significant change, as damage estimation has come to involve more sophisticated statistical techniques.[58] In one recent private antitrust case, for example, John

C. Beyer constructed a multiple regression model of an allegedly cartelized market to establish the existence and duration of the cartel's operation through which an overcharge exceeding 25 percent was estimated. Franklin M. Fisher, using the *same* regression model, but running it for different time periods, showed that defendants were *undercharging* during the period of the purported cartel.[59] A Chow test indicated Beyer's model had incorporated economic relations that had not remained stable during the time frame of the model. The entire episode illustrates both the growing use of econometrics in damage estimation and the pitfalls of the exercise. (See appendix A for a discussion of Beyer's model and Fisher's critique.)

Econometric models often perform poorly in making long-range forecasts. It is difficult to capture in a model the numerous changes normally occurring in an industry over the course of a period covered in a major antitrust action. Nevertheless, the application of such statistical techniques to the problem of damage estimation will likely continue in private actions. One can only imagine the reaction of Senator Sherman were he to learn that millions of dollars in Sherman Act damages would pivot on the application of a Chow test.

Diminished going-concern value. If a firm has suffered at the hands of an antitrust violator, the conventional wisdom has distinguished three approaches to estimating its damages: (1) determining the lost (net) profits of the business; (2) assessing the diminution of the firm's going-concern value; and (3) soliciting expert opinion regarding the injury.[60] There was a happier time for plaintiffs when they endeavored to collect for both lost future profits *and* the lower value of the firm. *Albrecht* v. *Herald Co.*, however, recognized that this involved double counting and eliminated the duality.[61]

Using method one or two should yield the same result. The value of a firm is the present value of a stream of profits plus the scrap value of the assets. Measuring the lower value of a firm should entail a dollar-for-dollar matching with the firm's lessened profits. The antitrust literature indicates, however, that litigants distinguish between the two approaches and are not indifferent about the choice.[62]

The measurement of damages caused by an antitrust violation is more complicated than the measurement in many tort cases because the damage to property is neither physical nor does it occur instantaneously. Moreover, during the time of injury, the plaintiff must seek to mitigate damages. The new learning has not contributed significantly to the methodology of damage estimation. The conventional methods, comparing the plaintiff's situation with that of another otherwise identical firm (the yardstick approach), or extrapolating from the plaintiff's performance during a different time frame (the projec-

22

tion approach), remain the two basic methods. With either method, the task is inherently case-by-case. The ability to select a yardstick firm in one private action may not exist in another. The task of estimating a plaintiff's sales, expenses, mitigation strategy, and its discount rate, based on its past experience, may be more tractable in some situations than others.

From an economic standpoint, it is difficult to conceive of injury to a firm's profit stream as substantial. This proposition does not rest on the difficulties in estimation. Rather it rests on the concept of opportunity cost and the legal obligation of plaintiffs to mitigate damages. If a physician, for example, were excluded from a particular hospital, and this were deemed an antitrust violation, the physician nevertheless must seek alternative employment under the obligation to mitigate damages.

A business firm, somehow prevented from buying a particular factor of production, is to seek substitute inputs or place its capital in another use. Unless the physician or the firm were making monopoly rents, the alternative uses of their capital, human or otherwise, should return an income stream comparable to that from which they were precluded.

The economic cost of the antitrust violation to them is not a lost stream of revenues. The loss, rather, is in the transaction costs incurred in shifting resources from one market (or use) to another. The loss parallels the reliance interest in contract damages, that is, the cost incurred in changing one's position.[63] For this reason alone, not to mention ease of damages estimation, a strong case can be made for compensating injured persons by the amount of these transaction costs, and these costs alone.[64] The new learning suggests that the lost-profit measure be abolished.

The judiciary and the new learning. Causal links between trends in judicial decisions and the scholarly literature are often difficult to discern. But consistent with the literature on private enforcement is a diminished eagerness on the part of courts to compensate plaintiffs through treble damages.

Traditionally, courts have narrowed the breadth of section 4 through the use of specialized standing rules. For many years, the focus of this analysis has been on the causal connection between the defendant's antitrust violation and the plaintiff's injury. Recently, courts have added another element to the standing analysis: whether a plaintiff has suffered an injury that "reflect[s] the anticompetitive effect of the violation or of anticompetitive acts made possible by the violation."[65]

From its inception, the Clayton Act has been ripe for such a

23

stricture on private recovery since a violation of this antitrust statute can occur without an actual lessening of competition. The law is prophylactic in its scope. A private plaintiff who proves the Clayton Act was violated may not have been injured financially if the lessening of competition had been stopped. There would be no "injury" in an economic sense, except for legal costs necessary to prove liability (presumably compensable under the act). Consequently, there should be no damages award for prophylactic suits.

This position was taken by the Court[66] in *Brunswick Corp.* v. *Pueblo Bowl-O-Mat Inc.,*[67] an opinion that has limited the standing opportunities for private plaintiffs. In this litigation, Brunswick had taken over the operation of bowling alleys that were delinquent on equipment loans made by Brunswick. The acquisition of the establishments constituted a section 7 violation. The plaintiff argued that had the defaulting bowling alleys not been acquired by Brunswick and instead had failed, its own bowling alleys would have been financially more successful. Thus, plaintiff was in effect complaining that defendants had preserved competitors.

The Court's position in *Brunswick* is that whenever a merger is undone because it may lessen competition, even parties actually injured by the merger can be denied the pursuit of multiple damages. For plaintiffs to recover treble damages in such litigation, they "must prove more than injury causally linked to an illegal presence in the market. Plaintiffs must prove *antitrust* injury, which is to say injury of the type the antitrust laws were intended to prevent and that flows from that which makes defendants' acts unlawful."[68]

In the parlance of the new learning, the requirement of antitrust injury would limit private actions to output-restricting violations and confine recovery of treble damages to those plaintiffs injured by the anticompetitive aspect of the violation. This would be of substantial aid in pursuing optimal deterrence under the framework of section 4. As evidenced by two recent cases, however, the Supreme Court does not appear to have embraced this approach to the doctrine of antitrust injury in all circumstances.

In *Blue Shield* v. *McCready,*[69] the Court applied the requirement of antitrust injury to an action alleging a violation of section 1 of the Sherman Act, indicating that *antitrust* injury is an important element of any private antitrust action. The plaintiff received medical insurance coverage under a Blue Shield health plan as part of the compensation from her employer. The plan included reimbursement for services provided by psychiatrists but did not cover treatment by psychologists. After being denied reimbursement for her psychologist's fees, the plaintiff brought a class action alleging an unlawful conspiracy between Blue Shield and a state psychiatrist association "to exclude and boycott clinical psychologists from receiving compensation under the Blue Shield plans."[70] She further alleged injuries equal to the amount of her psychologist's fees. The court held she had standing to maintain the suit under section 4 of the Clayton Act.

In its development of the doctrine of antitrust injury, *McCready* strays from the definition suggested by the new learning. The plaintiff's injuries did not flow from a restriction in output since she patronized a psychologist in spite of the alleged conspiracy. As the dissent pointed out:

> McCready alleges no anticompetitive effect upon herself. She does not allege that the conspiracy has affected the *availability* of the psychological services she sought and actually obtained. Nor does she allege that the conspiracy affected the *price* of the treatment she received. She does not allege that her injury was caused by any reduction in competition. . . .[71]

Nevertheless, the Court found McCready had suffered antitrust injury because "her injury was inextricably intertwined with the injury the conspirators sought to inflict on psychologists and the psychotherapy market."[72] Thus, the Court suggests that denial of standing for lack of antitrust injury should be limited to cases in which, as in *Brunswick*, the plaintiff's injuries are caused by increased competition.[73]

One year after *McCready*, the Court again addressed the issue of whether a party injured by an antitrust violation may recover treble damages. In *Associated General Contractors* v. *California State Council of Carpenters*, two carpentry unions filed a class action against an association of general contractors.[74] The unions alleged that the association had coerced certain landowners and general contractors to conduct business with nonunionized subcontractors. This behavior, they argued, injured unionized subcontractors, thereby indirectly injuring the unions. After discussing a broad set of considerations, the Court held that the unions were not eligible to recover under section 4. Since the use of nonunionized subcontractors increased competition in all markets involved, the denial of eligibility is in the new learning grain. But in analyzing whether the unions had standing, the Court identified several factors to be considered.

The requirement of antitrust injury and the traditional analysis of the causal connection between plaintiff's injury and the defendant's violation were among those factors considered. The Court, however, also considered the intent of the defendant, the risk of duplicate recovery or complex apportionment, the speculative nature of the injury, and whether there was a class of persons more directly injured by the violation who would likely be motivated to enforce the antitrust laws.[75] Thus, the Court adopted a balancing test to analyze eligibility under section 4.

In opting for a balancing approach to the standing issue, the Court stated "the infinite variety of claims that may arise make it virtually impossible to announce a black-letter rule that will dictate the result in every case."[76]

The open-ended balancing approach adopted by the Court makes it difficult for defendants confidently to determine ex ante who is eligible to sue them. This increases the danger that a private party will falsely claim anticompetitive behavior has taken place in hope that the defendant will pay some amount of money rather than go to trial. *Associated*'s approach to standing may increase the ability of private plaintiffs to exploit the misinformation effect.[77]

An additional problem with the Court's analysis is its discussion of the doctrine of antitrust injury. Although antitrust injury is cited as a relevant factor in determining standing under section 4, the Court does not specify whether the absence of antitrust injury is controlling. That is, after *Associated*, it is conceivable that a plaintiff who does not suffer antitrust injury may nonetheless be permitted to pursue treble damages if other relevant factors point toward permitting the action. This potential liberalizing of eligibility runs counter to the grain of the new learning.

The interplay between the new learning on private antitrust enforcement and the judiciary was manifested when the set of plaintiffs eligible to recover was reduced substantially by the Court's ruling that indirect purchasers could not recover treble damages (except under the narrowest of conditions).[78] The limitations *Illinois Brick* placed on private actions, its candid departure from the compensation goal, its obvious concern with ruinous awards, and its concern about litigating complex economic issues of cause and effect, are well known and oft debated.[79] The *Illinois Brick* noose was tightened when it was interpreted to deny standing to purchasers from fringe firms charging the cartel's price.[80] The judiciary's retreat from liberal recovery rules is again inconsistent with the goal of compensation, but recent empirical studies of the consequences of *Illinois Brick* give support to the correctness of that decision from the perspective of efficiency and deterrence.[81]

Some scholars have argued that courts now inhibit private enforcement through a more indirect route: to avoid awarding damages, and yet not to deny a plaintiff standing, they raise the original hurdle for the plaintiff, proof of liability.[82] The escalation is provoked by the concern that a finding of liability, coupled with damages multiples, will reduce the vigor of competition in the future by this defendant and others observing its fate.[83]

Courts also are requiring more rigorous estimates of damages. For example, damages awards may not be based on profits of a boom year projected to losses sustained during a recession.[84] Moreover, courts now take into account the strategic reaction of firms that would have taken place under competitive conditions, and the effect of these reactions on plaintiff's economic posture.[85] For example, a group of newspaper dealers who sued their newspaper because it had a resale price maintenance program were denied damages that were based upon the price increases they claimed they would have enacted absent the RPM program. The court reasoned that had these price increases been implemented by the dealers, the newspaper would have responded by integrating forward, eliminating them from the market.[86]

Courts are examining more closely the duration of the alleged damage period. In one recent case, an enterprising accountant projected lost profits of over $70 million for a period of twenty-seven years into the future. The jury agreed with the estimate. Reversing, the court of appeals found the award striking in that the company was newly formed, had no record of sales or profits, and was established to provide telephone service in an area not then developed.[87] The court threw out the award. The court may have been influenced by the fact that one plaintiff, who had put up $500 for the new venture, would have been entitled to damages exceeding $25 million.

Notwithstanding the intellectual energy expended in trying to refine the damages estimation process (whether for purposes of compensation *or* deterrence), the vast majority of damages paid as a result of antitrust litigation (or its threat) come through the settlement process. Here the decision calculus is based not on the niceties of deterrence or compensation but on the bargaining chips held by the opposing parties (which are largely determined by the legal rules).

Two things must be said about these settlements. First, they can be sizable. Their face value combined with the legal and managerial costs associated with attaining the settlement undoubtedly has a deterrence effect. For example, Levi Strauss & Co. paid $12.5 million for its vertical price restraints in California alone. The settlement, when challenged as being inadequate, was upheld, but not on the grounds that it matched any measure of consumer injury to the $1.4 million in claims for damages purportedly sustained on the sale of 37 million pairs of men's and boys' jeans. Rather, the award was upheld on the basis of legal obstacles to the recovery of the potential $240 million in damages.[88]

Second, courts are willing to accept ingenious and complex schemes to implement the distribution of these settlement amounts. In some cases, there may be a correlation between the recipient of the exaction and customers of the offending firm. For example, Cuisinart's settlement resulted in the company's issuing 50 percent discount coupons to class members. These could be redeemed through the purchase of additional Cuisinart products.[89] The coupons, worth up to $100 in their discount value, were mailed to former Cuisinart customers who earlier had mailed their warranty cards; the coupons were transferable and consequently had a cash value roughly equivalent to the alleged $32–$75 overcharge on Cuisinart products. In addition, notices of the discount coupons for those with proof of purchase were placed in magazines with circulations of several million.

But where products are low priced, and where proof of purchase with the defendant is costly to establish, negotiated settlements may forgo any serious attempt at either damage estimation or compensation of injured persons. For example, bakeries have been ordered to donate fresh baked goods to court-designated charities.[90] The proceeds from an antitrust settlement with broiler chicken processors went to Meals on Wheels, an organization providing hot meals to the elderly.[91] The monetary value of settlements such as these may have deterrence value,[92] though no attempt is made to calibrate this to an optimal sanction through the settlement process. The endeavor to match the award to those damaged, that is, to embrace the compensation goal, may even be disavowed in such settlements except as a wish.

The Supreme Court recently observed that "Congress did not intend to allow every person tangentially affected by an antitrust violation to maintain an action to recover threefold damages for the injury to his business or property."[93] To compensate every person whose economic well-being was diminished by market power would be impossible. But it is also the case that some persons unaffected by the exercise of market power (as consumers, as businesses, or as antitrust professionals) do benefit from private enforcement of antitrust and the awards and settlements it generates. One presumes Congress did not intend this transfer of wealth.

28

3
The New Learning on Contribution

The Question of Fairness

In the past decade the question of whether contribution should be a feature of antitrust enforcement has become a topic of lively concern.[94] Federal courts use a no-contribution rule. This means that one wrongdoer could be liable for all of the damages awarded in an antitrust proceeding. The court fixes the damages, deducts payments from any settling defendants (in order to prevent double recovery),[95] and permits the plaintiff to collect damages from other firms in any proportion he chooses. Under a no-contribution rule the defendant that pays more than its proportional share of the damages has no recourse against the other members of the cartel. Accordingly there is relatively great pressure on a defendant to settle early so as not to be exposed to the lion's share of the joint trebled damages.

The rule of no contribution raises questions of fairness and efficiency. As is usually the case when questions of equity are discussed, there is a lack of analytical precision. Easterbrook, Landes, and Posner dismiss the argument that a no-contribution rule is unfair on the grounds that the party claiming unfair treatment is himself a wrongdoer, and therefore protestations of inequity do not appeal to their "moral sense."[96] But it may take more to engage the moral sense of some economists than it would others with a lower threshold of outrage.

But that is not itself a "fair" response to Easterbrook, Landes, and Posner because they do not rest their argument entirely on such subjective considerations. They correctly point out that the wrongdoer could have avoided the risk by obeying the law. In addition, they argue that a rule of contribution would be costly, and its costs would fall on society as a whole while the benefits would inure to the wrongdoer. Indeed, the litigation costs of both parties under a contribution rule could also be discussed under the rubric of efficiency as well as equity, since they constitute reparations costs. Such costs are a deadweight loss to society. Any consideration of the costs and benefits of a contribution rule would have to take such considerations into account. But can a contribution rule be analyzed on grounds other than as a means of preventing unfairness? The emerging field of constitutional economics provides insights here.[97]

A Constitutional Perspective on Contribution

In order to guarantee an optimum number of law-abiding firms, it is necessary to accept the public bad of punishment. Unluckily punishment can be meted out only after the fact, while the institution selected for the purpose of deterring the illegal behavior is chosen before the fact. Observing a single firm paying the bulk of the damages while others involved in the cartel get off lightly will cause a loss of utility to members of society as their moral sense is injured. This may lead us to want to switch from a no-contribution to a contribution rule so that third parties will not suffer utility losses because some violators of the antitrust laws are minutely punished and others severely. Moreover, there is the problem of legal error. Some firms apprehended and convicted of price fixing will be falsely charged, and then innocent parties such as their shareholders and employees will suffer loss.

The recent surge of interest in establishing a contribution rule may be an increase in the subjective discount rate between present and future in which the preferred level of punishment falls as the observed punishment inflicts pain costs on the observers. This upward shift in the discount rate, however, simultaneously increases the number of violations, which leads, in turn, to a degenerative effect on law enforcement. After all, the decision to enter a cartel is a trade-off between anticipated future loss and present gain. Similarly a decision between a contribution rule and a no-contribution rule represents a trade-off between the present and the future, namely, of present utility losses against future deterrent effects. As the discount rate rises, the two effects work in the opposite direction: the present utility loss on society rises while the benefits of future deterrence fall. To the cartelist making the decision to enter a price-fixing conspiracy, the possibility of the future loss seems less important than the present gain. This means a simultaneous increase in violations and decrease in punishment. The system of order in antitrust enforcement may become unstable.[98]

To avoid this result economists have argued that our punishment system should be chosen strategically at the constitutional level of decision making and not at the post-constitutional stage. The policy should be selected independently of observed violations of the law, and the rules should be irrevocable once made.[99]

The present interest in a contribution rule after a no-contribution rule has been in force for so long may represent an expedient response to antitrust violations once they are committed.[100] The observation that it is "unfair" to inflict severe punishment on one violator of the antitrust laws while others get off lightly should not inform our decisions to abandon rationally chosen rules. The no-contribution rule might be interpreted as a rational decision made at the constitutional level of choice.[101]

Contribution and Efficiency: A Diagrammatic Approach

The verdict for or against a contribution rule will ultimately hinge more on our view of its efficiency than of its fairness. Not surprisingly, therefore, much more attention has been paid to that issue in the literature of economics. Under what condition is a no-contribution rule superior to a contribution rule in terms of its deterrent effect? And what are the relative costs of the two rules?[102] The analysis that follows presents, in their starkest form, the relevant issues involved in the contribution problem.

As long as the expected utility of monopoly profits is less than the anticipated damages, a firm will be deterred from illegal activity. Of course, there is no way of knowing whether the trebling of damages raises the expected loss to more than the aggregate gain in profits from a cartel. A firm pays damages only if it is detected and convicted of a violation. As we have seen, however, the utility of the expected profits will differ for different firms depending on the management's attitude toward risk. Economic analysis making use of the notion of varying risk attitudes indicates that a greater amount of deterrence will occur under a no-contribution rule than under any alternative.

Consider three different firms contemplating entering into an illegal price-fixing cartel. Firm A's management is risk averse, firm T's management is risk neutral, and firm P's management is risk preferring.[103] The relevant features of the contribution versus no-contribution rule can be summarized by the two-dimensional system of indifference curves shown in figure 2. The vertical axis measures the potential damages to be paid, and the horizontal axis measures the probability of paying damages. Unlike relative magnitudes in the usual construction of such diagrams, the magnitudes measured on each axis become smaller as they move away from the origin. The indifference curves depicted are iso-utility curves because they show,

FIGURE 2
HYPOTHETICAL INDIFFERENCE CURVES OF CORPORATE MANAGERS WITH VARYING ATTITUDES TOWARD RISK

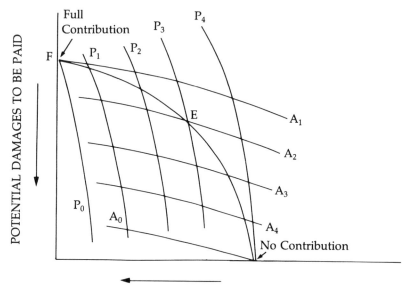

PROBABILITY OF PAYING DAMAGES

for a given manager, combinations of sums and probabilities of paying them, associated with a particular expected utility from the cartel profits. A movement along any curve indicates the amount by which a decrease in the magnitude on one axis must be compensated by an increase in the magnitude on the other axis to maintain a given degree of utility from cartelization. As the manager moves out to higher iso-expected utility curves—farther away from the origin—the greater the satisfaction achieved from monopoly profits and the greater the encouragement to enter a cartel agreement. The slopes of the curves depict the risk attitudes of the manager whose psychology is represented. The curve labeled *FN* is that of a risk-neutral manager because any movement along this curve leaves constant the expected value of the cartelist's profits, with any change in the probability of paying damages exactly compensated in terms of expected value by an opposite change in the potential damages to be paid. This iso-expected value curve is a rectangular hyperbola, which means that the manager with such a psychology is indifferent between paying, say, $100 and having a 50 percent chance of paying $200. The areas circumscribed under the curve have equal actuarial values and, by definition of an indifference curve, equal utilities. The curves labeled P are those of the risk-preferring manager and indicate by their slope that a relatively small reduction in the probability of paying damages must be compensated by a relatively large increase in the potential damages to be paid in order to maintain any given degree of expected utility from price-fixing behavior. Precisely the opposite attitude is depicted in the case of the curves labeled A, in which a relatively large reduction in the probability of paying damages needs to be compensated by only a relatively small increase in potential damages to be paid in order to maintain any given expected utility.

This simple diagram can shed considerable light on the question of the deterrent effects of contribution. Under a strict no-contribution rule the probability of paying damages is relatively small while the liability for large potential damages can be extremely high. This is true because, as we have seen, a plaintiff may decide to proceed against only one of the wrongdoers, and that firm would pay a disproportionately large share of the damages. A contribution rule is more reassuring to a firm since the sharing of damages awards will follow closely the sharing of the gains. Under a full-contribution rule, then, there is a larger probability of paying some relatively small amount of damages. This position is represented by point F on the vertical axis. Under a strict no-contribution rule, however, there is a relatively low probability of paying 100 percent of the damages. This position is represented by point N on the horizontal axis. Curve FN, therefore, represents the indifference curve of risk-neutral firm T. Curve FN (firm T's indifference curve) is intersected by the indifference curves of firms P and A; firm P's curves cutting firm T's curve from above (indicating its slope is greater than that of firm T), while curve A cuts the risk neutral indifference curve of firm T from below (indicating its slope is less than that of firm T).

Assume that, in terms of expenditures of resources, treble damages provisions, level of law enforcement, and the rule regarding sharing of damages, antitrust policy places society at point E, where the indifference curves of the managers of the three firms (who have different attitudes toward risk) cut each other.[104] Remember that the indifference curve of the risk-neutral firm is also, by definition, an iso-expected value curve since any movement along it will leave constant the expected value of the cartelist's profit, with any change in the probability of paying damages exactly compensated by an opposite movement in the expected value of the damages to be paid.

A decision to move from E toward a rule of full contribution would have no effect on the expected value of the firms' profits but would have immediate effects on the expected utility from those profits. The risk-averting firm would find itself moving northwest along iso-expected value curve *FN*, crossing ever higher indifference curves as it did so. In other words, it would be receiving increasing utility from the expected value of its ill-gotten gains. Under such a system the risk-averting firms can be predicted to engage in more illegal behavior. The risk-preferring firm, however, is in the opposite situation. The movement along *FN* causes it to fall to lower and lower indifference curves, meaning that *it* receives less satisfaction from a given expected value of monopoly profits. That being the case it will engage in less cartelization as a result of a movement to full contribution. The risk-neutral firm remains on the same indifference curve meaning that it will not change its behavior. Its "demand" for illegal monopoly profits will be the same under a no-contribution rule as it would be under a contribution rule, or any rule in between.

The adoption of a contribution rule, therefore, will have different effects depending on the risk attitudes of business managers. The greater the aversion to risk, the less the amount of cartel activity under a no-contribution rule. The greater the preference for risk, the greater the amount of cartelization under a no-contribution rule. What, then, is the new learning on risk attitudes of business managers?

Risk Attitudes of Managers

There is considerable evidence that managers are risk averse based on a number of industrial organization studies that indicate a new psychology dominates the attitudes of business leaders.[105] The work of Robert A. Gordon, Joseph Schumpeter, Robin Marris, Kenneth Boulding, Herbert A. Simon, Richard M. Cyert, and James G. March indicates that contemporary management wishes to avoid risk and uncertainty. Their studies are buttressed by the work of scholars in other disciplines such as William H. Whyte, Jr. and Antony Jay, who emphasize the importance of strict measures to conform, and constraints on individual expression in the modern corporation.

What these studies demonstrate is more than the assertion that businessmen are taking fewer risks than before. Obviously, taking fewer risks might simply mean that the odds have changed, and even risk preferrers will take fewer risks under greater odds.[106] But that misses the point. It is not that the *odds* have changed; it is that *attitudes* have changed. This involves a change in personality. The Carnegies, Rockefellers, and Firestones were not "organization men" like their later counterparts, the men in the gray flannel suits. Their tastes in

34

entertainment, display, food, housing, and art were different, or at least their consumption patterns were different. These changes in behavior are consistent with the hypothesis that attitudes toward risk have also changed.

Of course, the extent and intensity of risk aversion is still considered an unsettled question, but it is now part of the new learning that risk aversion characterizes corporate management.[107] This is the case even if shareholders are effectively risk neutral. The risk neutrality of shareholders is sometimes claimed because of the possibility that diversification of portfolios would make shareholders indifferent to any particular firm's activities. If the firm is under the control of shareholders it would be directed to maximize expected profits and would be indifferent to the utility to be derived from those profits. The firm would in effect be risk neutral. However, this conclusion is rejected by economists such as Polinsky and Shavell because of the transaction costs involved in the diversification of a portfolio, the superior information that might be possessed by some shareholders, and the cost of monitoring a firm's behavior.[108] As they argue, the aversion to risk of the firm's managers would ultimately control the firm's activities. Given the risk aversion of firms, our analysis predicts that less illegal behavior will occur under a system of no-contribution than under a system of contribution.[109]

This conclusion, however, does not make an unequivocal case for a no-contribution rule. As already noted, in a world of risk-averse corporate managers, no-contribution will lead to a higher degree of settlement before trial than will contribution. Since settling out of court would conserve judicial resources, it tends to strengthen the case for the no-contribution rule on efficiency grounds. The costs associated with nuisance suits, negotiations, and strategic bargaining would come into play more often, however, reducing the efficiency of the system. Moreover, a no-contribution rule could lead to over-deterrence by reducing some socially beneficial activities. This would be especially true where the offense of conspiracy is not clearly defined. On which side of the ledger the balance of effects would fall cannot be stated with certainty.

The strongest conclusion that can be made for retaining the no-contribution rule is that proponents of change have not made a persuasive case for change. Moreover, the new learning does formulate a clear-cut recommendation in favor of the no-contribution rule in the case of price fixing. If horizontal price fixing could be correctly defined, the problem of overdeterrence could not occur since horizontal price fixing has little if any social benefit.[110] The question of whether the optimal sanction is being enforced could be moot in this case.

4
Economic Costs of
Private Treble Damages Suits

The imposition of antitrust liability solely upon the alleged holder of market power generates three economic costs or inefficiencies.[111] These costs parallel those inherent in any system of strict liability where the offending party must pay compensation.

Perverse Incentives Effect

The first of the inefficiencies is that of perverse incentives. Under a system of treble damages, private parties may alter their economic behavior so as to contract the wealth of the economy. Under a system of treble damages, a customer of a cartel or monopolist has less motive to seek out substitutes. Indeed the customer may shop strategically, seeking to suffer damages in order to benefit from the collection of triple the amount of damages actually sustained. This is a variant of the moral hazard problem in insurance markets.[112]

It may appear at first that the perverse incentives effect should be labeled the "proper incentives effect" because it causes consumers to buy more of the monopolist's goods rather than less, reducing the deadweight loss resulting from monopoly. The monopolist would anticipate paying damages to those who do not substitute away from his product and treat those anticipated payments as a reduction in his profits. That, in turn, would lead to less monopolistic activity.

Obviously, if the deterrence incentives are strong enough to discourage monopoly in the first place, there could be no perverse incentives effect, for the latter exists only if a genuine violation of the antitrust laws has occurred. But this argument begs the question. When there is an overcharge by the undeterred monopolist cartel, if a customer overestimates the probability of a recovery of damages, there will clearly be overconsumption of the product, and the perverse incentives effect exists in its starkest form. This point is overlooked because people sometimes do not realize that too much of a monopolistic good can be purchased as well as too little. In either case inefficiency results.

The purchase of too much of a good also can occur if a person or firm substitutes toward a monopolist's product and away from a competitively produced product, not because the monopolist's product is superior but because private treble damages awards encourage such behavior. If individuals substitute away from a good they desire in favor of a substitute in order to take advantage of the possibility of damages recoveries, and if those potential awards do not deter the monopoly from overcharging, this encourages the employment of capital in less rather than more productive uses. The phenomenon is precisely parallel to the tax legislation that encourages the retention of corporate earnings even if the return that can be earned is less than that which the stockholder could earn by investing the funds elsewhere. The tax saving that encourages internal investment is analogous to the treble damage rewards that encourage overconsumption of a monopolized product.

The evidence of the extent and magnitude of the perverse incentives effect remains anecdotal, but it is conclusive of the reality of the phenomenon. One enterprising operator of a drive-in theater, for example, even kept two sets of books, one constructed to show low receipts (on which payments to its movie distributors were made) and another for purposes of its treble damages action against motion picture distributors.[113] As a matter of economic theory, the existence of perverse incentives should occur more frequently whenever the probability of conviction is high (putting the expected value of the award above the actual damage sustained).

The perverse incentives effect was first developed with regard to shopper behavior. Henry Butler has extended it to opportunistic behavior in restricted distribution contracts.[114] The basis of the opportunistic behavior of an antitrust plaintiff is a vertical contract into which an allegedly injured distributor voluntarily had entered. The fact that dealer terminations have constituted a sizable proportion of treble damages actions might be construed as indirect evidence of the perverse incentives effect. But as Butler is careful to explain, the mere number of lawsuits would never reveal the economic cost to society of this form of opportunistic behavior. Costs greater than the litigation come in the form of adjustments to the threat of opportunistic litigation, as manufacturers seek to avoid becoming victims of such lawsuits, either by greater investments in precontractual search or by finding alternative methods of distribution. When this occurs, the costs of the opportunistic behavior fall even upon those distributors who do not succumb to perverse incentives, through a lessening of the demand for their services.

In their analysis of private brands and national labels, Roger D. Blair and Yoram C. Peles argue that the *Borden* rule, in the context of private antitrust enforcement, encourages the perverse incentives effect.[115] A manufacturer producing a national brand and a private label has control only over the wholesale price differential between the two product lines. A purchaser of the national brand, hoping to use the antitrust laws against the manufacturer, could lower its retail prices of the national brand, thereby reducing the retail price differential between brands to an amount less than the wholesale amount. This would increase the manufacturer's antitrust exposure under *Borden*. The authors conclude, "the courts should consider market prices *generally* rather than *individual* prices of parties whose pricing decisions could be contaminated by perverse incentives."[116]

In response to the perverse incentives effect, courts now are more likely to expect plaintiffs to seek to mitigate their damages, a laudable situation.[117] In a monopolization case involving enormous damage claims, for example, where a jury found that plaintiff suffered $11.5 million in damages because of defendant's exclusionary behavior, the jury also "upheld Xerox's defense contention that SCM should reasonably have avoided all the 1969 exclusion claim damages by pursuing earlier litigation against Xerox."[118]

A retail maternity shop brought a private treble damages action against a manufacturer of infant strollers and its domestic distributorships. The plaintiff was a discounter who refused to repair or service the strollers, who balked at complying with the suggested retail price, and who was asked not to sell the strollers at a particular location already being serviced by another distributor. When these requests were made, the plaintiff reacted with abusive behavior, as if to provoke and clinch a refusal to sell by the manufacturer and its distributor. The unseemly behavior had its desired effect, setting up the plaintiff to sue for damages on charges of a concerted refusal to deal, horizontal and vertical price-fixing, and territorial restrictions, as well as charges of tying, monopolization, and price discrimination. The district court held for the manufacturer, recognizing that a ". . . businessman's churlish behavior should not be permitted to become an asset, enabling him to bootstrap himself onto an antitrust claim by having a reasonable businessman's refusal to deal with him be regarded as evidence of an illegal conspiracy."[119]

Another clear judicial recognition of the inefficiency of the perverse incentives effect occurred in *Golf City, Inc.* v. *Wilson Sporting Goods Co.*[120] Here a lower court had held that a retailer of golf merchandise in New Orleans, who had been deprived of "pro-line golf equipment," could have sold over a quarter million dollars worth of such equipment through the expenditure of only $6,000 in additional operating expenses. The appellate court found the figures to be erroneous but went on to state clearly that plaintiff "has a duty to mitigate damages."[121] In this instance, Golf City could have mitigated its damages and made many of the allegedly lost sales of pro-line equipment by purchasing "leaked" pro-line golf equipment from dealers authorized to purchase it or by increasing its sales of "store-line" golf equipment (which was available to it in the normal course of commerce). Unless Golf City was acting irrationally, its unrealized sales of golf equipment must have been the result of strategic behavior designed to run up its damages claims.

Misinformation Effect

The second of the inefficiencies, the misinformation effect, is the propensity for a private litigant to fabricate antitrust cases where no anticompetitive situation exists. The distinction between this effect and perverse incentives is that in the latter an actual trade restraint may exist (and provoke inefficient behavior). Misinformation effects (or nuisance suits) are provoked by the lure of treble damages but involve no actual trade restraints. To be sure, such suits could be brought by public enforcement agencies, themselves acting under misinformation or out of base motives. But they would not be provoked by the lure of treble damages.

The expected damages awards from litigation of this sort are nil (barring judicial error) should the case go to trial. But in the hope that defendants will pay some money rather than engage in the expense of litigation (and incur the chance of judicial error), private plaintiffs file their suits. The inefficiency is obvious: these costs are akin to a tax levied on the business sector by plaintiffs.

Collecting data on the extent and magnitude of the misinformation effect is problematic. Defendant firms and their counsel are reluctant to provide data on either the number of such settlements or the amounts of money involved for fear that the data will provoke the fabrication of additional lawsuits against their companies and clients, or stockholder reprisals, or both. The parallel to the misinformation effect in antitrust is the nuisance suit in personal injury cases. The extensive existence of such inefficiencies in that forum is commonly accepted.[122]

The magnitude of the misinformation effect and the cost it imposes on the economy is a function of the risk aversion of corporate management and the unpredictability of outcomes of antitrust litigation. Given the changing standards of liability in recent years in such areas as vertical restraints and discriminatory pricing, and the ambiguities of class certification and evidentiary standards even in per se areas of the law (such as price-fixing), most managements give serious thought to a financial settlement even when they are guiltless (or even when counsel places a high probability on a judicial determination of innocence).

The uncertainty is heightened by the use of juries in many private antitrust suits; the incentive to settle out of court is therefore greater as well. Moreover, in class actions, where the damage claims are often enormous, management's decision calculus may be to settle, not so much to remove a nuisance action against it, but as an *in terrorem* response to the repercussions of even a slim chance of losing.

A concern for the inefficiencies of the misinformation effect prompted the Federal Trade Commission to submit comments to the South Carolina legislature opposing legislation that would prohibit below-cost sales of motor fuel.[123] Under the proposed statute, successful plaintiffs could recover treble damages, exemplary damages, costs, and attorneys' fees and receive injunctive relief; violators faced jail sentences and fines as well. In addition to commenting that the legislation would protect dealer margins and result in higher fuel prices for consumers, the FTC staff predicted that the legislation would raise industry costs because of frivolous suits brought against sellers who are in compliance with the law but who are the low-price sellers in the market. The FTC also expressed a concern about the perverse incentives effect embedded in the proposed bill. Since the statute is not clear about precisely whose costs may not be undercut, opportunistic dealers could escalate their own costs, through increased advertising or salary expenses, for example, and then bring a spurious lawsuit for damages on the grounds that low-price sellers in their market were marketing motor fuels at prices less than the opportunistic dealers' costs.

The misinformation effect was heightened in the era of the "new antitrust strategy."[124] By this strategy, private plaintiffs seek not only the immediate economic reward of a pecuniary settlement but also the long-term benefit of inducing a defendant to "soften" the ardor of its rivalry. These may come in the form of less price competition, more favorable supply contracts, and other of what Austin calls the "noncompensatory goals" of private antitrust litigation; that is, to "intimidate defendants into modifying their conduct in a way favorable to the plaintiff."[125] This tactic falls neatly into the misinformation effect category of inefficiency.

The "new strategy" dovetails with the increasing willingness of business managers to sue members of their own club.[126] This change in attitude was spurred by the electrical equipment cases and ultimately by fear of shareholder reprisals if such damage actions were not filed. After tasting the fruit, and finding that it was good, managers ever since have been more disposed to become plaintiffs in antitrust litigation. Austin also credits the antitrust decisions of the Warren court and the risk aversion of defendant managers as impetuses for the new strategy.[127] Another example of the new strategy is the use of antitrust laws to thwart takeover attempts, where the private antitrust litigation constitutes a misinformation cost, but where the objective for the private plaintiff is a noncompensatory goal. Numerous cases could be chronicled in the past two decades in which firms have sued rivals with the objective of softening their competitive inroads or securing innovation predisclosure.[128] This variation on the misinformation effect was adroitly summarized by a former president of Control Data when discussing his company's lawsuit against IBM: "The decision to file a lawsuit in 1969, although difficult at the time, has proved to be one of the best management decisions in our history."[129]

Reparations Costs

There is a third inefficiency associated with private antitrust enforcement: reparations costs. While it is possible that society will incur costs of the misinformation effect even under a regime of public antitrust enforcement, reparations costs, like those associated with perverse incentives, are unique to private enforcement. These are the costs of resources used in determining and allocating damages (in contrast to public enforcement, which provides for no reparations). The compensation element of private enforcement extends the negotiation process in settled suits, requires greater judicial, legal, and clerical resources associated with the compensation task, and, because of the magnitude of some awards, induces more rent-seeking behavior on the part of plaintiffs (and their counsel). All this is a cost to society. Probably very little of the expenditure accomplishes actual reparations.

A measure of the problem is illustrated by the antibiotics case in which notice of a settlement fund was disseminated to over 50,000 drug wholesalers and retailers; claims were filed by less than 10 percent of them.[130] In the national class, in which users of tetracycline technically eligible for compensation numbered in the millions, Wheeler reports that "only 38,000 consumers filed claims against the settlement fund, . . . in spite of notice filed in every newspaper in the country."[131] Given the fine print of the notice, and the direct and time costs of proving purchase and securing reimbursement, what is surprising is how many *did* file claims. In class-action antitrust cases, where attorneys' fees of millions of dollars can be at stake, much of the courts' time in the reparations process must be spent on disputes over the intralawyer allocation of these fees.

Again, the magnitude of this inefficiency is difficult to assess. Robert Reich has estimated that the annual cost of the antitrust industry is $2.5 billion.[132] All of these resources devoted to reparations would be saved under a public-actions, fine-based regime, since the writing of a check to the U.S. Treasury uses minimal real resources. Even a system (such as that urged by Malcolm A. Wheeler) in which the government, and not private plaintiffs, brought suit for damages would substantially reduce the costs of reparations.[133] Obviously the reparations costs of getting persons compensated are reduced since the damages award goes to the Treasury (as a fine does). But in addition, by substituting a single plaintiff, the panel for multidistrict litigation and its attendant costs and the costs associated with the interaction among various plaintiffs' attorneys would be saved.

5

Reform of
Private Treble Damages Suits:
Procedural and Substantive

Legislative Alterations

In response to the growing disfavor with private treble damages enforcement, Congress in recent years has considered a number of modifications. The approach taken thus far has been a rearguard action rather than a frontal assault on private enforcement. But the effect has been to reduce the total damages available under the auspices of section 4 of the Clayton Act. Short of eliminating private treble damages actions in toto, the two alternative avenues for reducing their social cost is to lower the damages multiple or to decrease the number of offenses against which the multiple applies. The overall approach favored thus far has been a mixture of the two.

An illustration of the former is the Export Trading Company Act of 1982.[134] Export trading companies that have been certified by the Commerce Department, with the concurrence of the Department of Justice, are susceptible only to single damages for any antitrust violation within the scope of the certificate. Furthermore, a certified export trading company that successfully defends itself in an antitrust action can be compensated for court costs and its attorney's fees. This dampens any enthusiasm for vexatious litigation.

Similarly, for antitrust suits brought by foreign governments, Congress has limited recoveries to actual damages.[135] This legislation revised an earlier holding of the Court that foreign governments are entitled to recover treble damages under section 4 of the Clayton Act.[136]

For official conduct of local governments and their officials, Congress has eliminated all antitrust damages liability under sections 4, 4A, and 4C of the Clayton Act.[137] Suits for injunctive relief under section 16 and enforcement actions by government agencies are still available, however.

The treble damages avenue also has been foreclosed in cases involving joint research and development ventures. In the National Cooperative Research Act of 1984,[138] Congress provided protection for joint research and development endeavors. Most joint research and development projects would be compatible with federal antitrust laws, quite apart from this proposed legislation. But as William F. Baxter testified:

> Even though the risk of an incorrect legal decision may be small, that risk is exacerbated by the length, complexity and cost of antitrust suits and the fact that a successful claimant under the antitrust laws is automatically entitled to three times the damages actually suffered.[139]

Even the small probability of a private plaintiff's being successful, given the large potential cost exposure, will reduce the private sector's supply of joint research and development endeavors. Therefore the act limits liability to actual damages.

The Reagan administration's legislative proposals contained a more sweeping limitation of mandatory treble damages liability. The administration's proposal on treble damages was part of "a package of five legislative proposals which deal with all phases of the innovation process and seek to improve significantly the climate for the growth of technology."[140] Under this measure, plaintiffs would be entitled to treble damages recovery only when their claims arise from activities of the defendant that are "so plainly anticompetitive that they are deemed unreasonable and therefore illegal without elaborate study in each individual case as to the precise harm they have caused or the business justification for their use."[141] In short, treble damages liability would be limited to those activities that are per se illegal.[142]

Further Proposals for Reform

To ameliorate private enforcement, Posner suggests that when the violation is not concealable (as with mergers), multiple damages be disallowed.[143] Only single damages should be exacted. Trebling would be permitted only for those violations where the probability of detection is less than one—such as price-fixing. As a simple form of implementation, he would permit treble damage suits only by customers and suppliers of the defendant, never by rivals.

Blair's proposal parallels Posner's, except the character of the single damage measure is more precisely defined. He suggests that the actual damage measure include prejudgment interest and an allowance for inflation.[144] Thus a plaintiff winning a suit three years after injury would receive interest on the award, on the grounds that the defendant had the use of that money in the interim. And the award would be made in indexed dollars so that the plaintiff, in a time of inflation, is made whole. Presumably Blair would permit the same calculation during deflations to protect defendants. Increasing the damage estimate by both the rate of interest and the rate of inflation must be done carefully so as not to involve double counting.[145]

The restriction on trebling proposed by Phillip Areeda and Donald F. Turner is less severe than that of Posner or Blair. For those structural and behavioral situations in which they would commend private damage exactions, any multiplication of the award would be at the discretion of the judge.[146] The McKenzie study on industrial growth would reduce the damage multiple but would not allow judicial discretion.[147] This report of the Heritage Foundation recommends treble damages "only when the anticompetitive consequences of the business practice are not open to dispute." A maximum of single damages would be allowed in "rule of reason" cases. The Committee for Economic Development report, following Posner, calls for multiple damages only for per se concealable offenses and, following Areeda and Turner, recommends at a minimum that the multiple be at the discretion of the court.[148]

These proposals recognize what may not have been evident to the original supporters of the Sherman Act: antitrust violations vary in their economic consequences. Because of this, to permit private litigants to pursue every violation under the same damages multiple is a policy ripe for reform. A concealable violation that unabashedly causes economic harm, such as horizontal price-fixing, warrants a different deterrence measure than a practice such as tying, which is not readily concealed and whose allocative consequences are potentially benign.

Moreover, the track record of private antitrust suits is now available for scrutiny. It shows that many of these suits are disputes with little relationship to restoring or preserving competition. Many private antitrust actions, if they are disputes of legal concern, belong in the bailiwick of contract or tort law.[149] An example would be a termination dispute between a manufacturer and a distributor. Without reform of the private actions approach, they understandably become transformed by the lure of multiple damages from state court contract disputes to federal antitrust actions. The existence of these suits in the antitrust arena also suggests, as a minimum reform, a reduction of the damage multiple.

The Private versus Public Enforcement Mix

There is an emerging congruence between the Chicago and Harvard approaches to antitrust.[150] One illustration of this is their common disgruntlement with private treble damages enforcement and a revealed preference for public enforcement.

Richard Posner offers three reasons in support of a public actions approach: (1) the budgets of the antitrust agencies are relatively small, constraining the agencies in their choice of cases, whereas the private antitrust bar has a more "wild and woolly" disposition in case selection; (2) public actions may circumvent the problem of ineffective deterrence where customers are many; and (3) there is great difficulty in quantifying the effects of some antitrust violations and thus in constructing an optimal reward scheme for private enforcers.[151]

Areeda and Turner's list of negatives about private treble damages actions parallels Posner's. The ambiguity of the antitrust laws makes liability uncertain, so treble damages make no sense as a deterrent; private enforcement generally does not contribute to the development of the antitrust case law; and the prospects of treble damages, especially in class action suits, "trivialize" antitrust, making contract disputes into antitrust claims and subjecting defendants to lawsuits regarding conduct that has no socially harmful effects.[152] Areeda and Turner also would prohibit all damages actions against the horizontal restraint of "blameless" monopolization.[153] In comparing government suits for equitable relief with private suits, they write that "the key difference between them [is] that the government suit is much more likely to reflect a thorough assessment and dispassionate conclusions regarding the public interest."[154] This assessment produces a stronger disposition to public enforcement.[155]

Robert Bork doubts even the detective abilities of private plaintiffs, arguing instead that one of the shortcomings of antitrust enforcement is the paucity of public resources devoted to uncovering price-fixing conspiracies. His recommendation is for a dispersed and decentralized (if not expanded) Antitrust Division.[156] Rather than concentrating the personnel in Washington, D.C., Bork suggests numerous field offices for this agency, not only to uncover localized price-fixing but also to allow the antitrust authorities to give more attention to economic predation carried out through misuse of courts and administrative agencies.

Elzinga and Breit support a totally public action approach to antitrust on the ground that antitrust fits the characteristics of a public good, and voluntary actions are not likely to offer the optimal amount of enforcement.[157] Of course, to argue that antitrust violations are an example of market failure is not to clinch the case for government over private actions. Economists have devised numerous schemes to privatize the provision of a public good for the market failure of pollution. But thus far there has been no resolution of the inefficiencies associated with private enforcement.[158] In the absence of any sensible method of making the public good of antitrust enforcement available through private enforcement, Elzinga and Breit would replace the entire damage-induced private actions approach with a system of fines (well in excess of current levels).[159] This proposal would eliminate the perverse incentives and misinformation effects and reparations costs. Public enforcement has the advantage of separating incentives for enforcement from the penalty itself. The amount of the fine therefore can be altered without in any way affecting the resources going into detection and conviction of violators.

Empirical support for the institution of a high fine with no change in enforcement resources, public or private, comes from the recent study by Block, Feinstein, and Nold of highway bid-rigging. They found that the number of cases brought against bid-rigging (a proxy for the probability of detection and conviction) did not appear to alter the level of price-fixing in highway construction. What did have an effect in reducing collusion was the severity of the penalty.[160] This suggests that the colluders were risk averse, meaning that the combination of a high fine with a low probability of detection and conviction caused more disutility than a lower fine coupled with greater resources devoted to enforcement that yielded the same expected cost to the price fixer. The congenial feature of this risk characteristic, of course, is that it enables high levels of deterrence against price-fixing at relatively low cost.

Roderick Dorman offers still another reason for avoiding reliance on private enforcement. He argues that under a system of pure private enforcement, where plaintiffs are entrepreneurial in their intent, convictions would be difficult to obtain (and therefore deterrence levels would be suboptimal).[161] If jury members are aware that the damages award will go not to injured persons but rather to a self-interested private attorney general who has no business connection with the violation, they will be unlikely to convict. This may, however, be more an argument against jury trials in antitrust than an argument against purely private enforcement.

A defender of private actions, Irwin Stelzer, cites an American Bar Association study that revealed that of the 352 private antitrust cases brought in the Southern District of New York between 1973 and

1978, almost three-fourths of these involved vertical conduct (for instance, dealer terminations, tying requirements, resale price maintenance).[162] He argues from this that private suits such as these, challenging practices ignored by the federal and state antitrust agencies, are the only recourse plaintiffs have. But his evidence adduced in favor of private enforcement turns badly on itself. Such violations fall predominantly under the category of what the new learning deems efficient offenses. From an economic standpoint, society does not want these activities deterred, especially in a world of scarce judicial resources.

After his review of the strategies and consequences of private treble damages enforcement, Arthur Austin, although not optimistic about the repeal of private enforcement, concluded that the government should have exclusive responsibility for antitrust enforcement.[163] As a minimal legislative alternative to scrapping private enforcement, Austin proposed that any noncompensatory settlements between private antitrust disputants be submitted to the Antitrust Division for review prior to court approval. A less sweeping proposal was made by Kenneth Dam. After reviewing the efficiency aspects of class action antitrust cases, he recommended a sizable increase in the fines resulting from successful government actions.[164] Private antitrust, in his view, should be subordinated by prohibiting private litigation once a public proceeding has begun. Private enforcement could commence only if filed before a public action.

A purely public actions approach does not mean that private parties could not or would not have input into the operations of the Department of Justice and the Federal Trade Commission. As is the case now, parties that see themselves as injured by antitrust violations would have positive incentives to promote investigations and the filing of complaints, and even to involve themselves in the relief and remedy process. If, in the absence of treble damages, the flow of useful information to the agencies ceased (an unlikely situation), an economic inducement could be offered for information critical to the filing of a successful government suit. But with the private actions avenue closed, the flow of information to the public agencies probably would increase. Any concern that an obstinate agency might refuse to consider a meritorious investigation or complaint urged upon it by a private person could be alleviated by allowing an administrative or judicial review of the purported lack of investigation or complaint. Of course, no one knows precisely the incentive structure of the public enforcement bureaucracy. In principle, they could be motivated to achieve optimal enforcement in a way impossible with our present system of private actions.

Incidence of Attorney Fees

The task of streamlining antitrust enforcement in such a way that real attorneys' fees are reduced is not addressed in this paper. The new learning on private antitrust has, however, considered the incentive structure of the current legal framework that asymmetrically awards attorneys' fees to successful plaintiffs from defendant coffers but does not require unsuccessful plaintiffs to compensate defendants for their litigation expenses.

Gary Becker has suggested that if the cost imposed upon those who brought unsuccessful antitrust suits were high enough (perhaps through multiple attorney fees that unsuccessful plaintiffs would be required to pay to defendants), then the filing of misinformation suits would be deterred. Yet the threat of such penalties on risk-averse potential plaintiffs may discourage some output-expanding lawsuits. After a review of the incentive effects of awarding attorney fees, Warren Schwartz concluded that the "rules should be neutral toward both plaintiff and defendant" in the distribution of litigation costs.[165] One of the most respected treatises on the U.S. antitrust laws, that of Neale and Goyder, suggests a more limited reform: that courts require plaintiffs to pay attorney fees only for suits brought "in bad faith or vexatiously."[166] Their limitation only to bad-faith suits is unwarranted. The "English rule," in which any suit won by defendants would have reasonable attorney fees compensated by plaintiffs, would be preferable—just as defendants are responsible for the reasonable attorney fees of prevailing plaintiffs.

Juries in Private Actions

In jury trials for treble damages, the jury estimates the economic value of the injury to the plaintiff. The competing damage theories of the adversaries inevitably provide the jury with a broad range from which to choose. Under the present system, the jury's assessment, of course, is trebled. Thus any overestimate on the part of a jury is magnified by that multiple. There is a propensity on the part of those juries that are unaware of the trebling provision to assess larger damages than what they perceive was the plaintiff's loss, while juries aware of the trebling provision reduce their awards in order to lessen the windfall.[167] Since juries generally are *not* informed by the court that the damage determination they make will be trebled, and because section 4 of the Clayton Act is not posted in every household, jurors have expressed dismay upon learning that what they believed was already a generous award in an antitrust case was going to be trebled.[168] The upshot is that the search for the optimal damage award may be thwarted by the variable of the jury's knowledge or ignorance of the damage multiple, a circumstance that could differ from case to case.[169]

It is possible to conceive of modifications to the jury system to ameliorate this situation. Courts could uniformly inform juries of the trebling provision or adopt special jury instructions designed to prevent any attempts by uninformed juries to enlarge their damage assessments for reasons of equity. These reforms would be procedural.

The more substantive reform is to abolish the use of juries in antitrust cases, especially if efficiency standards are to hold sway. This would apply not only to private actions, in which the issue of damage estimation may be complex, but to public actions as well, in that the question of liability in either type of case can be prolonged and technical. In one complex antitrust trial that led to a deadlocked jury, the foreman was asked by the judge whether such cases should be tried by juries. The man responded, "If you can find a jury that's both a computer technician, a lawyer, an economist, knows all about the stuff, yes, I think you could have a qualified jury, but we don't know anything about that."[170] Other jurors in this trial were polled, and some concluded that complex antitrust cases might better be tried by the judge than by a jury. To remove such litigation from the realm of juries is not to belittle their intelligence but rather to recognize the economic, technological, accounting, and statistical complexity of antitrust.[171]

6
Other Penalties:
Incarceration and Fines

The private actions sanctions are of course only one part of the assortment of policy instruments that were explicitly provided in the Sherman Act. In addition to treble damages paid to injured private parties, there are public action devices for penalizing antitrust violations. They are: (1) incarceration; (2) financial penalties paid to the state; and (3) injunctive directives such as the corporate surgery of dissolution, divorcement, and divestiture. From the standpoint of economic analysis, all of these penalties affect the expected utility from anticompetitive behavior, which in turn depends on the businessman's attitude toward risk. As we saw in our discussion of the contribution issue, the more averse the business manager is to risk, the more he will be deterred by any given reduction in the expected value of monopoly profits resulting from increased risk. The more of a risk lover a manager happens to be, the less will he be deterred by any reduction in the expected value of monopoly profits resulting from increased risk. The attitude toward risk determines the utility or satisfaction that one gets from expected profits. Antitrust weaponry can be effective only if consistent with these attitudes.

In recent years each of these instruments has been subjected to analysis that has led to a reconsideration of the conventional wisdom regarding their efficacy. Just as in the case of private antitrust enforcement, dissatisfaction with these public action tools has also led to a revision of previously accepted beliefs and a concomitant new learning, albeit without as much analysis or consensus as in the case of the treble damages sanction.

Incarceration

The relationship between monopoly and incarceration is known to many generations of youngsters familiar with the famous Parker

Brothers game Monopoly. The connection made derives from the chance card that says "Go directly to jail, do not pass Go, do not collect $200." In reality, of course, jailing of corporate executives who are convicted of violating the antitrust laws is not as direct a consequence as devotees of the game of Monopoly might have come to expect.

During the first fifty years of antitrust enforcement under the Sherman Act, of 252 criminal prosecutions only twenty-four resulted in jail sentences, and only eleven of those involved businessmen (the rest were trade-union leaders). Moreover, ten of the eleven cases involved acts of violence, threats, and other forms of intimidation, and the remaining jail sentence was suspended. From 1940 to 1955 only eleven prison sentences were imposed, and in almost every case the sentences were suspended. It was not until 1959 that a prison sentence was imposed for price-fixing alone, in which no acts of violence or union misconduct were involved. In that case the court imposed a ninety-day prison term on four individuals and fined each $5,000.[172]

The year 1960 saw the advent of the notorious electrical equipment cases.[173] By 1966, at the termination of these cases, seven company officials had received thirty-day jail terms, a fact that led a number of observers to believe that a new era had been ushered in.[174] But this belief proved premature. From 1966 to 1973 only eighteen cases resulted in the imposition of jail sentences. In only seven of these was time actually served, as compared to the 1955–1965 period when twenty-six cases resulted in jail sentences with only six actually served.[175]

The year 1974 was a watershed in the history of antitrust enforcement legislation. In that year President Gerald Ford signed into law the first major reform in the antitrust laws in over twenty years: the Antitrust Procedures and Penalties Act.[176] This law changed violations of the Sherman Act from misdemeanors to felonies, increased the maximum jail term from one to three years, and raised the maximum fine from $50,000 to $1 million for corporations and from $50,000 to $100,000 for individuals.

Since this law went into effect, somewhat higher fines and stiffer jail sentences have been meted out.[177] During the period covered by Elzinga and Breit in their study of incarceration for antitrust violations, roughly 5 percent of the convictions resulted in jail terms.[178] Since the passage of the Antitrust Procedures and Penalties Act, 20 percent of the criminal convictions have resulted in incarceration.[179] Table 1 summarizes the cases involving penal sanctions since the Antitrust Procedures and Penalties Act was passed. This act clearly has had an effect on the courts' willingness to impose jail terms for antitrust violations, although seldom has the maximum term allowed under the law been imposed.

The four antitrust penalties (reparations in the form of treble damages, incarceration, fines, and injunctive relief) on the surface appear to differ greatly. But as Gary Becker has noted:

> The cost of different punishments to an offender can be made comparable by converting them into their monetary equivalent or worth, which, of course, is directly measured only for fines. For example, the cost of an imprisonment is the discounted sum of the earnings foregone and the value placed on the restrictions in consumption and freedom.[180]

In the case of fines and reparations the monetary counterpart of the penalties imposed is directly measured. Incarceration also can be collapsed into its pecuniary equivalent.

Is there a realistic monetary equivalent for incarceration? One might suppose the ignominy, deprivation of liberty, inconvenience, and humiliation associated with a jail term would be incomparable to any other penalty imposed for antitrust violations. During the hearings over the Antitrust Procedures and Penalties Act in 1974, Congressman John Seiberling of Ohio argued that:

> If there is any one thing from my own experience that has made the enforcement of the antitrust laws much more meaningful, it was when courts started sentencing corporate executives to jail, because if there is one thing most corporate executives . . . do not like it is having a criminal label attached to them for the rest of their lives and having reputations of having served time in jail.[181]

The notion that incarceration is a very special weapon was emphasized by Assistant Attorney General J. Paul McGrath. In his initial policy speech on his priorities for the Antitrust Division, he stressed incarceration for convicted price fixers, saying that such individuals "are thieves and felons" and belong "behind bars."[182]

But the new learning on incarceration stresses the Becker approach, to wit, that jail sentences can in fact be converted into an equivalent monetary sum. Richard Posner, for example, argues that all white-collar criminals should be punished only by monetary exactions—by fines rather than by imprisonment (unless imprisonment is necessary to coerce the payment of the fine). He used a cost-benefit analysis. The net social cost of fining is limited to the cost of collecting the fine and shows up almost entirely on the benefit side of the social ledger. Imprisonment, however, has no comparable social revenue.

TABLE 1

Criminal Sanctions—Imprisonment 1975–1984

Year	Number of Criminal Cases	Number of Convictions	Number of Imprisonments Imposed		Length of Sentence	Characteristics of Case
			Cases	Persons		
1975	25	23	2	1	45 days	Price-fixing
				1	30 days	Bid-rigging
1976	24	21	4	1	1–15 days, work release	Price-fixing
				2	30 days	Price-fixing
				1	30 days	Customer and territory allocation
				1	45 days	
				2	4 months	Price-fixing
1977	25	24	8	2	1 year	Bid-rigging
				1	18 months	Bid-rigging
				1	2 years	Bid-rigging
				1	30 months	
				1	30 days	Price-fixing
				1	60 days	Price-fixing
				2	30 days	Price-fixing
				2	20 days	
				1	60 days	Bid-rigging
				1	45 days	Customer allocation

Year				No.	Length	Violation
1978	30	28	4	5	30 days	Price-fixing
				5	90 days	
				1	15 days	Customer allocation, bid-rigging
				4	90 days	Bid-rigging
				1	1 year and 1 day	
				2	30 days	Bid-rigging
				1	3 years	
				1	45 days	Price-fixing
				3	30 days	
				2	60 days	
1979	17	16	2	2	90 days	Price-fixing
				2	10 days	Bid-rigging, customer allocation
1975–1979	*121*	*112*	*20*	*51*		
1980	23	14	6	1	2 months	Bid-rigging
				4	2 months	Bid-rigging
				9	1 month	
				1	71 days	
				1	45 days	
				1	75 days	
				1	24 months	Bid-rigging
				2	1 month	
				3	2 months	
				2	2 months	Bid-rigging
				3	1 month	Price-fixing
				3	45 days	Price-fixing, customer allocation

(Table continues)

TABLE 1 (continued)

Year	Number of Criminal Cases	Number of Convictions	Number of Imprisonments Imposed		Length of Sentence	Characteristics of Case
			Cases	Persons		
1981	7	6	0			
1982	15	6	3	1	120 days	Bid-rigging
				1	2 months	Bid-rigging
				1	90 days	Bid-rigging
				1	60 days	Bid-rigging
1983	44	18	5	1	1 month	Bid-rigging
				1	45 days	Bid-rigging
				1	200 days	Bid-rigging
				1	6.5 months	Price-fixing, bid-rigging
				1	14 days	Bid-rigging
1984	27	12	2	1	30 days	Price-fixing
				1	75 days	Bid-rigging
1980–1984	116	56	16	42		
TOTAL	403	318	45	120		

NOTE: Suspended and remitted prison sentences are excluded.
SOURCE: Joseph C. Gallo, Joseph L. Craycraft, and Steven C. Bush, "Guess Who Came to Dinner: An Empirical Study of Federal Antitrust Enforcement for the Period 1963–1984," *Review of Industrial Organization*, vol. II, no. 2, 1985.

It involves considerable sums spent on confining and maintaining prisoners, causing only a cost with no revenue or output offset.[183]

Although it seems obvious that fines are less costly to society (when the offender can pay the fine) than imprisonment, is it also true that fines have an equivalent deterrent value? As table 1 demonstrates, antitrust offenders are not punished by long prison terms. Given these low levels of imprisonment, it is likely there is a fine that is equivalent to the existing prison sentences in the amount of disutility that it imposes on offenders. In addition, jail sentences have little deterrent effect because of their infrequent use. There is an understandable reluctance of juries and judges to believe that antitrust violators merit jail or that the chief corporate culprits have been identified. This is a purely pragmatic consideration which, when combined with the new learning on incarceration vis-à-vis fines, makes incarceration an inferior penalty.[184]

Fines

Under the original Sherman Act, the maximum fine was $5,000 per count, which could be levied against corporations, individuals, or both. Although over the years Congress often considered bills to augment this picayune penalty, it did not increase the fine until 1955 when the penalty was raised to a maximum of $50,000. Given the returns from monopoly power in a cartel, however, and the probability of detection and conviction of less than one, this maximum fine was of little deterrent effect. In the electrical equipment conspiracy cases the average fine imposed upon each corporate defendant was a mere $16,500.[185] The passage of the Antitrust Procedures and Penalties Act at the end of 1974, which elevated the maximum fine, has had considerable effect on the average level of fines, which have increased 325 percent since its passage.[186] Since the maximum fine that could be levied increased twentyfold, the full possibility of using fines as a deterrent has not yet been exhausted (see table 2). Moreover, the level of real fines has fallen dramatically since 1980.

Even though fines are still minuscule under the Sherman Act, the actual level of fines to which corporations and individuals might be subject is much larger than a reading of the antitrust laws by themselves would reveal. In 1984 Congress passed the Criminal Fine Enforcement Act, which went into effect on January 1, 1985.[187] This law imposes a new fine structure that raises the permissible exaction for an individual convicted under a Sherman Act violation from $100,000 to $250,000. What is more, the statute contains a double damages provision allowing the United States to secure a fine equal to twice

TABLE 2
DEPARTMENT OF JUSTICE CASES: CRIMINAL SANCTIONS—FINES, 1963–1984

Year	Number of Convictions	Number of Fines Imposed	Aggregate Fines (in dollars)	Average Fine per Case (in dollars)	Aggregate Fines (in 1972 dollars)	Average Fines (in 1972 dollars)
1963	8	8	690,500	86,313	963,444	120,431
1964	14	14	1,333,450	95,246	1,832,417	133,096
1965	7	7	1,408,150	201,164	1,893,693	270,527
1966	16	16	2,047,650	127,978	2,667,600	166,725
1967	13	11	1,164,707	96,792	1,346,708	122,429
1968	15	15	1,172,750	78,183	1,420,826	94,721
1969	1	1	130,000	130,000	149,787	149,787
1965–1969	*52*	*50*	*5,923,257*	*116,465*	*7,478,614*	*149,572*
1970	9	9	761,800	84,644	833,024	92,558
1971	8	8	577,500	72,188	601,500	75,188
1972	19	17	1,480,500	87,058	1,480,500	87,058
1973	17	17	2,164,700	127,335	2,048,160	120,478
1974	25	25	3,164,500	126,580	2,753,655	110,146
1970–1974	*78*	*76*	*8,149,000*	*107,224*	*7,716,839*	*101,537*

1975	23	23	2,121,600	92,244	1,689,710	73,408
1976	21	20	5,313,130	265,657	4,021,747	201,088
1977	24	23	8,700,750	378,294	6,222,377	270,539
1978	28	27	11,832,375	438,236	7,885,622	292,060
1979	16	14	12,380,500	884,321	7,605,824	541,133
1975–1979	*112*	*107*	*40,348,355*	*377,087*	*27,425,280*	*256,311*
1980	14	13	15,570,000	1,197,692	8,726,000	671,277
1981	6	6	5,316,000	866,000	2,724,198	454,033
1982	6	5	3,514,200	702,840	1,698,666	339,733
1983	18	16	6,010,000	375,625	2,786,665	174,166
1984	12	12	2,318,500	193,208	1,042,116	86,843
1980–1984	*56*	*52*	*32,728,700*	*629,398*	*16,977,645*	*326,493*
TOTAL	320	307	89,073,262	290,141	62,394,239	203,239

SOURCE: Joseph C. Gallo, Joseph L. Craycraft, and Steven C. Bush, "Guess Who Came to Dinner: An Empirical Study of Federal Antitrust Enforcement for the Period 1963–1984," *Review of Industrial Organization*, vol. II, no. 2, 1985.

the gross monetary gain from the violation, or twice the loss to another person, whichever is greater. Since the Justice Department has not yet invoked its new power to seek damages, it is too early to analyze the practical effect of this law on Sherman Act criminal cases. At the 1984 spring meeting of the American Bar Association, however, a moderator of a panel on Criminal Practices and Procedure, Robert E. Cooper, called the Criminal Fine Enforcement Act a "ticking time bomb" for antitrust lawyers.[188]

The advantage of levying fines, as we have seen, is clear and compelling. The marginal social cost of imposing a higher instead of a lower fine is virtually zero. Congress or the courts could alter the level of the fine at no cost since imposing the higher fine requires no more resources than charging a lower fine. Not only is the fine cheaper to administer than any other of the antitrust penalties, it involves a transfer of revenue from the wrongdoer to the state.

7
Conclusion

The sanctions and remedies of antitrust deserve the same careful attention as the process of case selection itself. An optimal enforcement policy must consider both the economic behavior of a defendant before prosecution and the defendant's behavior after prosecution. It is a healthy sign of antitrust scholarship that both prongs of antitrust enforcement are being examined.

An economic assessment of the costs and benefits of the public sector's weapons of fines and incarceration comes down in favor of the former. A monetary exaction paid to the state can have the same deterrent consequences as a jail sentence, and without the social costs accompanying imprisonment. Reducing reliance on jails and increasing reliance on fines would constitute an economic reform of the antitrust arsenal. The case for raising the level of the fine above its current level is a strong one, especially if reform of the private sector's antitrust weaponry is enacted.

There is considerable agreement that the private treble damages antitrust action is ripe for reform. Support for this assessment has a broad foundation, but its firmest grounding can be found in the new learning. Jonathan Rose, a former director of the Justice Department's Office of Legal Policy remarked that in the mid-1970s even the questioning of this weapon in the arsenal of antitrust could only "have been held in the basement of the Chicago Law School attended by about four or five economic zealots."[189] Rose's statement was made at a recent session of the American Bar Association that was evaluating alternatives to mandatory trebling.

The prevailing consensus is that the current statutory construction needs changing, though the proposals for reform are somewhat diverse. They range from complete reliance upon public enforcement to recommendations that effectively would lower the damage multiple, raise the requirements for eligibility to recover damages, and preclude private actions in specified circumstances. Secondary reforms would award attorneys' fees to either prevailing party. These proposals, while varied, are more notable for their similarity. All of the proposals are endeavors to seriously limit the scope of what the Court has called private attorneys general.

As notable as the new learning on private antitrust (and possibly not unrelated to it) are the changing attitudes of the courts toward private antitrust enforcement. As courts have recognized the inefficiencies of private actions, and yet have been constrained by the Clayton Act's mandatory trebling provision, their response has been an indirect reduction of the reach and pecuniary magnitude of private actions. This has taken the form of stricter standards regarding liability, standing, and damage estimation. As has been suggested here, the failure of Congress to offer significant remedy for the inefficiencies of private enforcement eventually may be rectified by the course of judicial reaction.

Appendix

In the corrugated container opt-out case, the expert economic witness for the plaintiffs, Dr. John C. Beyer, developed an econometric model of the corrugated container industry.[1] From this, he concluded the existence of a conspiracy and estimated the resulting overcharge paid by plaintiffs. The model embraced seven factors allegedly determining the price of corrugated containers and sheets from which Beyer estimated the relationship between these (the independent variables) and the price of corrugated containers (the dependent variable). This estimate was made using the ordinary least squares method of regression analysis as applied to data from January 1963 to December 1974. Beyer assumed collusive activities were taking place during this period. Once he established the relationship between the independent variables and the price of corrugated containers, he projected forward to determine what prices would be in the subsequent period based upon these relationships.

The results of the regression analysis are shown in figure A–1. Beyer proposed the existence of three stages of collusive effects. During the first stage, from January 1963 to December 1975, the full force of the cartel was affecting purchasers of corrugated containers. The second stage, referred to as the transition period, is from January 1975 to late 1978. Beyer argued that during this period, although most collusive activity had ceased, remnants of the cartel were still affecting purchasers.[2] The competitive period is the third and final period; it runs from January 1979 to August 1981. Using this time frame as a base, Beyer calculated the average annual overcharge due to collusive activities. It was not insubstantial: 26.1 percent. The figure was derived by taking the percentage difference during this period between the forecasted price and the average national price based on a price index developed from data gathered by the Fibre Box Association.

The Beyer testimony was concluded with the statement that the analysis was not dependent on specific evidence that the defendants fixed the prices charged these plaintiffs. "The conclusions rest in terms of what the underlying economic data tell us actually occurred in the

FIGURE A–1

FBA CORRUGATED CONTAINER PRICE INDEX:
ACTUAL VERSUS SIMULATED
(December 1974 = 100)

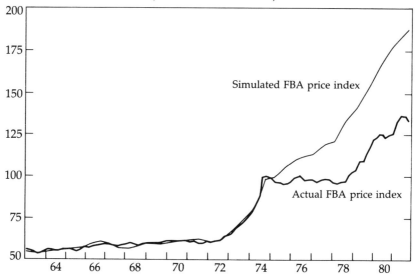

NOTE: Beyer's model, estimation period: 1963:1 to 1971:7.

industry."[3] The approach used was a "during and after" one, but with a twist. Instead of comparing later prices with an earlier period known to be competitive, earlier prices were compared with later ones presumed to be competitive.

Three extraordinary events took place in the corrugated container industry from August 1971 to the end of 1974. These events were: (1) the imposition of price controls in August 1971 and their subsequent release toward the end of 1974; (2) the energy crisis that began at the end of 1973; and (3) a shortage of linerboard (an input into the production of corrugated containers) during 1973 and 1974. If a model is truly a structural model, adequately and accurately accounting for these events, it should generate substantially the same numbers if one estimates the model before these events took place and then begins forecasting forward in August 1971 rather than in January 1975. In other words, if the model accounts for these events, then taking them out or leaving them in should not make a difference.

To test this, the Beyer model was fit to the period from January 1963 to July 1971 and then used to project the price of corrugated container out to August 1981. This was done in the opt-out case by defendants' economist Franklin M. Fisher.[4] Based on that fit, one can test whether the Beyer model accounts for these events. This is shown in figure A–2. As the figure indicates, rather than tracking the actual price to 1975 and then reflecting the overcharge that would have occurred had the alleged conspiracy continued (as in figure A–1), it meanders off and predicts that there would have been an *undercharge* if the alleged conspiracy had continued.

The Beyer model probably was driven by the extraordinary events that took place from August 1971 to the end of 1974. This can be tested econometrically by a Chow test.[5] When the Chow test was run, comparing the periods January 1963–July 1971 (before price controls) and August 1971–December 1974 (imposition and subsequent release of price controls), it indicated that the differences in the regression coefficients would not be this great, if attributed to chance fluctuations, except in about one in a million times. From this, Fisher concluded that the Beyer model was not a structural model that explains the entire period; he argued "it is the forcing of that special period

FIGURE A–2

FBA CORRUGATED CONTAINER PRICE INDEX:
ACTUAL VERSUS SIMULATED
(December 1974 = 100)

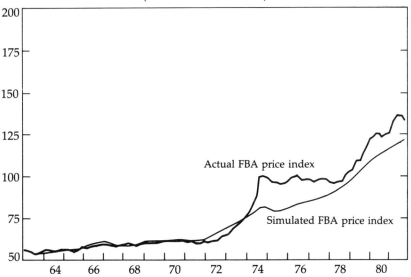

NOTE: Beyer's model, estimation period: 1963:1 to 1975:1.

in with the early one, which generates the results with the 26 percent overcharge."[6]

Fisher used the Chow test to further criticize the Beyer model by applying it to the alleged transition period. Beyer had stated in his testimony that the transition period was easy to discern; it started where the predicted price line begins to diverge from the actual price line (January 1975) and ends where the divergence between the two lines has stabilized (late 1978). According to Beyer, during the transition period the effect of the conspiracy is gradually mitigated by competition. When the lines begin to move in a parallel fashion, all the lingering effects of collusion are gone, and the competitive period has been reached.

But when Fisher applied the Chow test to the Beyer data, it offered no convincing evidence that there was a statistical difference between the two periods. In other words, the results of the Chow test showed the same equation could likely explain prices in the years 1975 through 1981. Given this result, Fisher then fit the Beyer model to the data of that period, February 1975–August 1981, and projected backwards into the alleged collusive period (see figure A–3). Once again the simulated price *exceeded* the actual (and allegedly conspiratorial) price level. Fisher concluded his testimony by stating: "Econometric modeling, even if done properly, is probably not a useful or reliable way to estimate an overcharge in this case."[7]

Notes

1. The model was virtually the same as that used earlier in the class action. See "Final Report Concerning Expert Testimony on Damages," In Re Corrugated Container Litigation, Civ. Action MDL 310, Dep. Ex. 6700-1, March 31, 1980.

2. This was a result of continuing contracts negotiated during the non-competitive period, some of which had automatic escalators. During the transition period these waning effects are gradually mitigated by competition, and eventually the competitive period is reached.

3. Beyer transcript, December 15, 1982, p. 132.

4. See Fisher transcript, In Re Corrugated Container Antitrust Litigation, February 8, 1983. There were several criticisms of the Beyer model that reflect the growing emphasis on econometrics in damage estimation, but they are not summarized here.

5. The Chow test is used to determine whether economic relationships have remained stable in two different periods of time. That is, it is designed to test whether the regression coefficients (or a subset of them) are the same for two samples. If not, the estimated coefficients lose their reliability. The test is performed by fitting (estimating the regression coefficients) the same

FIGURE A-3
FBA CORRUGATED CONTAINER PRICE INDEX:
ACTUAL VERSUS SIMULATED
(December 1974 = 100)

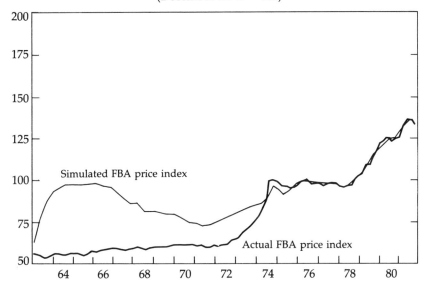

NOTE: Beyer's model, estimation period: 1975:2 to 1981:8.

equation to two different time periods. While there will almost always be numerically different results, the Chow test estimates how likely it is that the difference observed can be due to chance fluctuations.

6. Fisher transcript, p. 431.

7. Fisher transcript, p. 440. See also his "Multiple Regression in Legal Proceedings," *Columbia Law Review*, vol. 80 (May 1980), pp. 702–36 (a cautious assessment of the utility of such models); Daniel L. Rubinfeld and Peter O. Steiner, "Quantitative Methods in Antitrust Litigation," *Law and Contemporary Problems*, vol. 46 (Autumn 1983), pp. 69–141.

Notes to Text

We are indebted to Alden F. Abbott, Phillip Areeda, William F. Baxter, Roger D. Blair, Yale Brozen, James M. Clabault, Joseph L. Craycraft, Joseph C. Gallo, William H. Page, Laura Bennett Peterson, A. Mitchell Polinsky, Edward A. Synder, Pablo T. Spiller, and Gordon Spivack for their helpful comments. Rita Miller, James R. Pagano, and Kevin Terhaar provided research assistance, and Peggy Claytor was exceptionally diligent in getting the manuscript into its final form. Responsibility for remaining errors is the authors'.

1. A part of this study is drawn from William Breit and Kenneth G. Elzinga, "Private Antitrust Enforcement: The New Learning," *Journal of Law & Economics*, vol. 28 (May 1985), pp. 405–43.

2. Richard A. Posner, "The Chicago School of Antitrust Analysis," *University of Pennsylvania Law Review*, vol. 127 (April 1979), pp. 925–48; Study of the Antitrust Treble Damage Penalty, *Report*, Committee on the Judiciary, H.R. 98th Congress, 2d session, February 1984, p. 16.

3. Richard A. Posner, *Antitrust Law: An Economic Perspective* (Chicago: University of Chicago Press, 1976), p. 35.

4. "From Economic Theory to Harvard Don," *New York Times*, April 1, 1984, section III, p. 4.

5. William Breit and Kenneth G. Elzinga, "Antitrust Enforcement and Economic Efficiency: The Uneasy Case for Treble Damages," *Journal of Law & Economics*, vol. 17 (October 1974), pp. 329–56. For a more recent critique in this journal, see Frank H. Easterbrook, "Detrebling Antitrust Damages," *Journal of Law & Economics*, vol. 28 (May 1985), pp. 445–67, and Breit and Elzinga, "Private Antitrust Enforcement: The New Learning."

6. Phillip Areeda and Donald F. Turner, *Antitrust Law* (Boston: Little, Brown & Co., 1978), pp. 149–51.

7. "Congressional Developments in Antitrust," *Antitrust Law Journal*, vol. 50 (April 1981), pp. 59–65 at p. 63.

8. *Congressional Record*, April 11, 1983, p. E1473.

9. "Study of the Antitrust Treble Damage Penalty."

10. Lawrence Vold, "Are Threefold Damages Under the Antitrust Act Penal or Compensatory?" *Kentucky Law Journal*, vol. 28 (January 1940), pp. 117–59.

11. William M. Landes gives a clear example of this point. "Optimal Sanctions for Antitrust Violations," *University of Chicago Law Review*, vol. 50 (Spring 1983), pp. 652–78 at pp. 653–55.

12. Gary S. Becker, "Crime and Punishment: An Economic Approach," *Journal of Political Economy*, vol. 76 (March/April 1968), pp. 169–217.

13. See William Breit and Kenneth G. Elzinga, "Antitrust Penalties and Attitudes Toward Risk: An Economic Analysis," *Harvard Law Review*, vol. 86 (February 1973), pp. 693–713. The importance of attitudes toward risk in analyzing antitrust policy reappears in the discussion of one of the most recent issues to arise in antitrust enforcement, that of contribution. See chapter 3. For an analysis that takes into account the cost of catching violators as well as their risk attitudes, see A. Mitchell Polinsky and Steven Shavell, "The

Optimal Tradeoff Between the Probability and Magnitude of Fines," *American Economic Review*, vol. 69 (December 1979), pp. 880–91.

14. The importance of deterrence as the goal of antitrust in the new learning was stated boldly by Frank H. Easterbrook: "Deterrence is thus the first, and probably the only, goal of antitrust penalties. If awarding damages to an injured party also compensates him, that is just a pleasant byproduct." See his "Predatory Strategies and Counterstrategies," *University of Chicago Law Review*, vol. 48 (Spring 1981), pp. 263–337 at p. 319. For a contrary view stressing compensation for antitrust victims and incarceration for violators (a perspective that is not part of the new learning), see Roger D. Blair, "Antitrust Penalties: Deterrence and Compensation," *Utah Law Review*, vol. 1980 (1980), pp. 57–72.

15. Polinsky and Shavell, "The Optimal Tradeoff."

16. See, for an example, Donald Dewey, "Information, Entry, and Welfare: The Case for Collusion," *American Economic Review*, vol. 69 (September 1979), pp. 587–94.

17. See Michael K. Block and Joseph Gregory Sidak, "The Cost of Antitrust Deterrence: Why Not Hang a Price Fixer Now and Then?" *Georgetown Law Journal*, vol. 68 (June 1980), pp. 1131–39 at p. 1138, giving credit to Warren F. Schwartz.

18. The concept of expected value is basic to understanding choices that are made under conditions of uncertainty. Expected value is the weighted sum of the values of possible events where the weights are the probabilities of the occurrence of each event. For example, if a price fixer faced a 10 percent chance of being caught and fined a million dollars and a 90 percent chance of being undetected and going unfined, $100,000 would be the expected value of the fine faced by the price fixer.

19. Richard A. Posner has pointed out that optimal punishment through fines or damages, in driving a wedge between the fine and the social cost of the crime, causes the punishment to deviate from proportionality to the gravity of the crime. Therefore it is anathema to retributivists who believe that it is morally fitting that wrongdoers should suffer in proportion to the severity of the offense. The economic rationale for punishment, which attempts to make wrongdoers internalize the social costs of their activities, is therefore not necessarily consistent with a retributivist rationale for punishment. Moreover, it is not necessarily consistent with a strict deterrence theory of punishment, which holds that the incidence of crime should be reduced to zero. See Richard A. Posner, "Retribution and Related Concepts of Punishment," *Journal of Legal Studies*, vol. 9 (January 1980), pp. 71–92 at pp. 73–74.

20. Kenneth G. Elzinga and William Breit, *The Antitrust Penalties: A Study in Law and Economics* (New Haven, Conn.: Yale University Press, 1976), pp. 7–13.

21. Li Way Lee, "Some Models of Antitrust Enforcement," *Southern Economic Journal*, vol. 47 (July 1980), pp. 147–55.

22. Robert W. Feinberg, "On Optimal Antitrust Enforcement: Comment," *Southern Economic Journal*, vol. 48 (April 1982), pp. 1095–97.

23. Easterbrook, "Predatory Strategies," p. 322.

24. William H. Page, "Antitrust Damages and Economic Efficiency: An Approach to Antitrust Injury," *University of Chicago Law Review*, vol. 47 (Spring 1980), pp. 467–505 at p. 479. This is also the position taken by Joseph G. Sidak in "Rethinking Antitrust Damages," *Stanford Law Review*, vol. 33 (January 1981), pp. 329–52 at p. 340, in which the size of monopoly profits is suggested as the appropriate sanction. For those unfamiliar with the technical vocabulary of economics, a word of explanation regarding the concept of "consumers' surplus" and its significance might be in order. The consumers' surplus is the difference between how much a consumer pays for a product and how much he would be willing to pay rather than go without it. This surplus is an index of well-being. If it could be measured accurately, it would provide a test of the amount of welfare the economy generates. What would be required is a list of the maximum prices a consumer would be willing to pay for each unit of a good, compared with the price he actually pays. In figure 1–1 consumers' surplus at price P_0 for Q_0 units of the commodity would be approximated by the triangle CEP_0. When the price rises to P_1 as a result of the collusive agreement among the firms, the loss in consumers' surplus is the area of the trapezoid P_1DEP_0. Since part of this loss (the rectangle P_1DRP_0) is simply a transfer to the cartelists, the *net* loss to society is triangle DER, since this area represents that amount of the consumers' surplus that is totally lost to society—neither the consumers nor the cartelists receive it. In the literature of economics it is sometimes referred to as "deadweight loss."

25. For an illustration, see Landes, "Optimal Sanctions for Antitrust Violations," pp. 658–61.

26. Warren F. Schwartz, "An Overview of the Economics of Antitrust Enforcement," *Georgetown Law Journal*, vol. 68 (June 1980), pp. 1075–1102 at pp. 1081–85.

27. Richard A. Posner and Frank H. Easterbrook, *Antitrust: Cases, Economic Notes and Other Materials* (St. Paul, Minn.: West Publishing Co., 2d ed. 1981), p. 550.

28. "Optimal Sanctions for Antitrust Violations," p. 656.

29. Ibid., p. 661.

30. Breit and Elzinga, "Antitrust Enforcement and Economic Efficiency."

31. Gary S. Becker and George J. Stigler, "Law Enforcement, Malfeasance, and the Compensation of Enforcers," *Journal of Legal Studies*, vol. 3 (January 1974), pp. 1–18. For a recent defense of private enforcement, see David Friedman, "Efficient Institutions for the Private Enforcement of Law," *Journal of Legal Studies*, vol. 13 (June 1984), pp. 379–97.

32. William M. Landes and Richard A. Posner, "The Private Enforcement of Law," *Journal of Legal Studies*, vol. 4 (June 1975), pp. 1–46.

33. James C. Ellert, "Antitrust Enforcement and the Behaviour of Stock Prices" (Ph.D. diss., University of Chicago, 1975).

34. Ibid., pp. 128–29.

35. Malcolm R. Burns, "The Competitive Effects of Trust-Busting: A Portfolio Analysis," *Journal of Political Economy*, vol. 85 (August 1977), pp. 717–

39.

36. Kenneth D. Garbade, William L. Silber, and Lawrence J. White, "Market Reaction to the Filing of Antitrust Suits: An Aggregate and Cross-sectional Analysis," *Review of Economics and Statistics*, vol. 64 (November 1982), pp. 686–91.

37. Dosoung Choi and George C. Philippatos, "Financial Consequences of Antitrust Enforcement," *Review of Economics and Statistics*, vol. 65 (August 1983), pp. 501–06.

38. Michael K. Block, Frederick C. Nold, and Joseph G. Sidak, "The Deterrent Effect of Antitrust Enforcement," *Journal of Political Economy*, vol. 89 (June 1981), pp. 429–45.

39. Michael K. Block, Jonathan S. Feinstein, and Frederick C. Nold, "The Effectiveness of Recent U.S. Government Criminal Antitrust Enforcement Efforts in the Construction Industry," forthcoming in *Internationale Forschungsergebnisse auf dem Gebiet der Wirtschaftskriminalität* (International Results of Research in Economic Crime).

40. Edward A. Snyder, "Defensive Effort and Efficient Enforcement" (Ph.D. diss., University of Chicago, 1984).

41. "The Economics of Antitrust Enforcement: Theory and Measurement," *Georgetown Law Journal*, vol. 68 (June 1980), pp. 1121–30.

42. It is difficult, arguably impossible, to measure accurately the deterrence of a given antitrust penalty, mainly because the extent of undetected violations is unknown. Also, the current mix of public-private enforcement makes it difficult to distinguish the proportion of deterrence due to a particular penalty. Progress in that direction will depend in part on the existence of better data. The importance of a data base has been recognized by such groups as the Business Roundtable, the National Association of Manufacturers, and the Chamber of Commerce. As a result of discussions with representatives of these organizations, Robert Pitofsky, Thomas Krattenmaker, and Steven Salop of the Georgetown University Law Center have developed a study that is intended to provide a data base that would cast light on the present enforcement system and any alternatives. From these data it is hoped that future researchers can make more reliable estimates of the "costs, risks and rewards of private antitrust actions." See Thomas Krattenmaker, Robert Pitofsky, and Steven Salop, "Memorandum: Treble Damages Research Project," July 28, 1983. See also, *A Proposal for Data Collection and Analysis*, Georgetown University Law Center (December 20, 1983).

43. Page, "Antitrust Damages," p. 468.

44. Clayton Act, chap. 323, 4, 38 Stat. 730, 731 (1914) (Current version at 15 U.S.C. 15(a)(1982)).

45. Ibid.

46. See our section in this book, "The Judiciary and the New Learning" and accompanying notes.

47. William H. Page, "The Scope of Liability for Antitrust Violations," (unpublished manuscript), 1984.

48. Phillip Areeda, "Antitrust Violations Without Damage Recoveries," *Harvard Law Review*, vol. 89 (April 1976), pp. 1127–39; Page, "Antitrust Dam-

ages"; Page, "The Scope of Liability"; Sidak, "Rethinking Antitrust Damages."

49. The concept of antitrust injury began with Areeda, ibid. The term was coined a year later, however, in Brunswick Corp. v. Pueblo Bowl-O-Mat, 429 U.S. 477 (1977). Since this decision, scholars have molded and refined the meaning of antitrust injury in attempting to achieve optimal deterrence under section 4.

50. As Page put it, "just as economic analysis of the effects of various practices on efficiency should guide the development of the rule of reason in the formulation of substantive rules, so the same tools should give the content to the concept of antitrust injury." "Antitrust Damages," p. 472.

51. To determine whether a plaintiff's injuries are caused by the anticompetitive aspect of the violation, Page suggests asking "whether the harm alleged varies in direct proportion to the inefficiency associated with the practice." See "The Scope of Liability," p. 20. Standing alone, this test may not limit damage awards to the optimal penalty. Page argues, however, that when it is used in conjunction with the Illinois Brick doctrine and a standing analysis designed to confine recovery to the "most efficient class or classes of plaintiffs from among those that have suffered antitrust injury," optimal deterrence can be approximated. Ibid., pp. 12–13.

52. Ibid., p. 21.

53. For a summary of who has standing and who does not, and the conflicting views of the various circuit courts, see Note, "Private Antitrust Standing: A Survey and Analysis of the Law after Associated General," Washington University Law Quarterly, vol. 61, (Winter 1984), pp. 1069–1101. The premier source is Areeda and Turner, Antitrust Law, pp. 160–227.

54. Page, "The Scope of Liability," p. 25; In Re Industrial Gas Antitrust Litigation, 681 F.2d 514 (7th Cir. 1982), cert. denied, 460 U.S. 1016 (1983). But see, Eleanor M. Fox, "Standing: Should Standing be Granted to the Most Efficient Enforcer?—Whistle Blowers, Takeover Targets and Competitor-Plaintiffs" (unpublished manuscript); Ostrofe v. H. S. Crocker Co., 670 F.2d 1378 (9th Cir. 1982), on remand, 740 F.2d 739 (9th Cir. 1984).

55. Richard A. Posner, Antitrust: Cases, Economic Notes, and Other Materials (St. Paul, Minn.: West Publishing Co., 1974), p. 149 as quoted in Page, "Antitrust Damages," p. 475.

56. See Story Parchment Co. v. Paterson Parchment, 282 U.S. 555, 563 (1931) and Bigelow v. RKO Radio Pictures, 327 U.S. 251, 264 (1946). "The cases have drawn a distinction between the quantum of proof necessary to show the fact as distinguished from the amount of damage; the burden as to the former is the more stringent one. In other words, the fact of an injury must be shown before the jury is allowed to estimate the amount of damage." Flintkote v. Lysfjord, 246 F.2d 368, 392 (9th Cir. 1957). Some cases have allowed "proof of losses which border on the speculative." Ford Motor Co. v. Webster Auto Sales, Inc. 361 F.2d 874, 887 (1966), quoting Momand v. Universal Film Exchanges, Inc. 172 F.2d 37, 43 (1st Cir. 1948). When experts are used in the damage estimation process, they have been "allowed some economic imagination so long as it does not become fantasy." Terrell v.

Household Goods Carriers' Bureau, 494 F.2d 16, 25 (5th Cir. 1974).

57. See, for example, Charles A. Bane, *The Electrical Equipment Conspiracies* (New York: Federal Legal Publications, 1973), pp. 508–09; for an illustration drawn from a retail industry see, Federal Trade Commission, Bureau of Economics, *Economic Papers 1966–1969*, no. 136 (n.d.).

58. See In Re Corrugated Container Litigation, Civ. Action MDL 310, Dep. Ex. 6700-1, March 31, 1980, for the model and the testimony of John C. Beyer, plaintiffs' expert, transcript, December 15, 1982, and Franklin M. Fisher, defendants' expert, transcript, February 8, 1983, and Defendants' Exhibits 1351-1352-1353.

59. Fisher concluded his testimony by stating: "Econometric modeling, even if done properly, is probably not a useful or reliable way to estimate an overcharge in this case." Ibid., p. 440. See also Fisher's "Multiple Regression in Legal Proceedings," *Columbia Law Review*, vol. 80 (May 1980), pp. 702–36 (a cautious assessment of the utility of such models); Daniel L. Rubinfeld and Peter O. Steiner, "Quantitative Methods in Antitrust Litigation," *Law and Contemporary Problems*, vol. 46 (Autumn 1983), pp. 69–141.

60. Expert opinion (unless it is the expertise of the haruspex) should not count as a distinct approach. The expert in economics, accounting, or finance must look to either lost profits or the lessened value of the business in assessing the damage estimate.

61. 390 U.S. 145, 154 (1968).

62. The choice for lost profits appears to arise from the methods acceptable to the courts in estimating market value. Generally courts will hear evidence only on factors affecting the value of a firm to a "willing buyer." Thus losses in nontransferable goodwill are not compensable as a reduction in a firm's market value. But they may be recovered under the lost profits measure. See Note, "Private Treble Damage Antitrust Suits: Measures of Damages for Destruction of All or Part of a Business," *Harvard Law Review*, Vol. 80 (May 1967), pp. 1566–1586. The two methods may be combined, one as a check against the other, or, in the case of a destroyed business, lost profits used as the damage measure during the period of destruction and diminution of going concern value after the cessation of the business. See Heatransfer Corp. v. Volkswagenwerk, A. G., 553 F.2d 964 (5th Cir. 1977).

63. John D. Calamari and Joseph M. Perillo, *The Law of Contracts* (St. Paul, Minn.: West Publishing Co., 2d ed. 1977), p. 522.

64. See Areeda and Turner, *Antitrust Law*, pp. 233–34; Note, "Unestablished Businesses and Treble Damage Recovery Under Section Four of the Clayton Act," *University of Chicago Law Review*, vol. 49 (Fall 1983), pp. 1076–97.

65. Brunswick Corp. v. Pueblo Bowl-O-Mat, 429 U.S. 477, 489 (1977). For a full discussion of the development of antitrust standing see Comment, "A Farewell to Arms: The Implementation of a Policy-Based Standing Analysis in Antitrust Treble Damages Actions," *California Law Review*, vol. 72 (May 1984), pp. 437–76 at pp. 441–56.

66. The same position was taken earlier by Areeda, "Antitrust Violations Without Damage Recoveries," pp. 1129–30. The influence of Areeda's article

upon the Court's reversing NBO Industries Treadway Cos. v. Brunswick Corp., 523 F.2d 961 (1975) is probable.

67. 429 U.S. 477 (1977).

68. Ibid. at p. 489 (emphasis in original).

69. 457 U.S. 465 (1982).

70. Ibid., p. 470.

71. Ibid., p. 489 (Rehnquist, J., dissenting).

72. Ibid., p. 484.

73. Ibid., pp. 482–83.

74. 459 U.S. 519 (1983).

75. Ibid., pp. 545–46.

76. Ibid., p. 536.

77. See Breit and Elzinga, "Antitrust Enforcement and Economic Efficiency," pp. 340–42 and chapter 4 of this study.

78. Illinois Brick Co. v. Illinois, 431 U.S. 720 (1977). The exception for an indirect purchaser is when it buys under a preexisting, fixed-quantity, cost-plus contract.

79. Compare William M. Landes and Richard A. Posner, "Should Indirect Purchasers Have Standing to Sue Under the Antitrust Laws? An Economic Analysis of the Rule of *Illinois Brick*," *University of Chicago Law Review*, vol. 46 (Spring 1979), pp. 602–35, and Robert G. Harris and Lawrence A. Sullivan, "Passing on the Monopoly Overcharge: A Comprehensive Policy Analysis," *University of Pennsylvania Law Review*, vol. 128 (December 1979), pp. 269–360.

80. Mid-West Paper Products Co. v. Continental Group, Inc., 596 F.2d 573 (3d Cir. 1979). See also, Note, "Standing of Purchasers From Nonconspirators to Challenge Price-Fixing Conspiracy," *Harvard Law Review*, vol. 93 (January 1980), pp. 598–607.

81. See Edward A. Snyder, "Efficient Assignment of Rights to Sue for Antitrust Damages," *Journal of Law & Economics*, vol. 28 (May 1985), pp. 469–82; Jon M. Joyce and Robert H. McGuckin, "Assignment of Rights to Sue Under *Illinois Brick*: An Empirical Assessment," U.S. Department of Justice Economic Policy Office Discussion Paper #EPO 85-6 (April 9, 1985).

82. Joseph L. McEntee, Jr., "Damages for Victims of Monopolization: The Berkey Photo and SCM Experience," *Antitrust Law Journal*, vol. 49 (March 1980), pp. 1303–10 at p. 1305.

83. Berkey Photo Inc. v. Eastman Kodak Co., 603 F.2d 163 (2d Cir. 1979); Northeastern Telephone Co. v. American Telephone and Telegraph Co., 651 F.2d 76 (2d Cir. 1981).

84. R. S. E. Inc. v. Pennsy Supply Inc., 523 F. Supp. 954, 964–968 (M.D. Pa. 1981). The court also rejected a profit estimate of the plaintiff that was based on different years for different segments of the firm's business such that when summed yielded a rate of return larger than the firm had ever made in its history. The estimated profit figure was 25.3 percent, soberly attested as to its reasonableness even though all rival firms averaged a 3.2 percent rate of return.

85. Ibid. at p. 966 regarding need to incorporate the reactions of other firms in damage estimation.

86. Knutson v. Daily Review, Inc. 468 F. Supp. 226, 240 (1979). Judge Renfrew did award each plaintiff $3 in nominal damages.

87. Mid-Texas Communication v. American Telephone and Telegraph Co., 615 F.2d 1372, 1391 (5th Cir. 1980).

88. "Court Sustains $12.5 Million Settlement of Price Fixing Claims Against Levi Strauss," *BNA Antitrust & Trade Regulation Report*, vol. 45 (December 15, 1983), p. 977.

89. "Cuisinart's Settlement Gets Stamp of Approval," *BNA Antitrust & Trade Regulation Report*, vol. 45 (November 10, 1983), p. 756.

90. "Bakers Sentenced For Price Fixing Must Give Sweets to Needy Organizations," *BNA Antitrust & Trade Regulation Report*, vol. 44 (May 12, 1983), pp. 961–63.

91. "Colorado Uses Chicken Settlement to Fund Meals-On-Wheels for Elderly," *BNA Antitrust & Trade Regulation Report*, vol. 44 (June 16, 1983), p. 1187.

92. One wonders at the ultimate cost to Cuisinart of its discount coupons. Their redemption, necessarily involving the purchase of additional Cuisinart products, is not a net loss to the company as was the case with Levi-Strauss. The losers in the settlement were the rivals of Cuisinart!

93. Blue Shield v. McCready, 457 U.S. 465 (1982).

94. See, for example, Note, "Contribution in Private Antitrust Actions," *Harvard Law Review*, vol. 93 (May 1980), pp. 1540–61. Note, "Contribution for Antitrust Codefendants," *Virginia Law Review*, vol. 66 (May 1980), pp. 797–825; Frank H. Easterbrook, William M. Landes, and Richard A. Posner, "Contribution Among Antitrust Defendants: A Legal and Economic Analysis," *Journal of Law & Economics*, vol. 23 (October 1980), pp. 331–70; A. Mitchell Polinsky and Steven Shavell, "Contribution and Claim Reduction among Antitrust Defendants: An Economic Analysis," *Stanford Law Review*, vol. 33 (February 1981), pp. 447–71; and, see generally, U.S. Congress, Senate, Subcommittee on Antitrust, Monopoly, and Business Rights, *Antitrust Equal Enforcement Act of 1979: Hearings on S. 1468 before the Subcommittee on Antitrust, Monopoly, and Business Rights of the Senate Judiciary Committee*, 96th Congress, 1st session, 1979.

95. See Zenith Radio Corp. v. Hazeltine Research Inc., 401 U.S. 321, 348 (1971).

96. Easterbrook, Landes, and Posner, "Contribution among Defendants," p. 339.

97. See Richard B. McKenzie, ed., *Constitutional Economics: Containing the Economic Powers of Government* (Lexington, Mass.: Lexington Books, 1984), particularly the papers by James M. Buchanan, Robert H. Bork, and Karen I. Vaughn for a summary of this approach.

98. This analysis follows closely that of James M. Buchanan, *The Limits of Liberty: Between Anarchy and Leviathan* (Chicago: University of Chicago Press, 1975), pp. 130–46.

99. Ibid., p. 136.

100. An example of this state of mind is indicated by the following remarks of former Attorney General Griffin Bell at the American Bar Association annual meetings in 1983: "The system went wrong when we had joint and

several liability coupled with the class action concept. The result is the possibility of huge damages. You get more damages than anyone can pay. In the *Mead* case in Houston, a case I was involved in, the *ad damnum* clause indicated that it would be $800 million. That would be what they would owe because they had to make up for what others who settled did not pay. . . . They had a choice. They could have paid. They could have settled. But to me that is anti-American not to be able to go to trial if you think you have a right, if you think you have a fair defense. That is what the problem is, and no one will address that." Joe Sims, ed., "New Approaches to Antitrust Damages: The Alternatives to Mandatory Trebling," *The Business Lawyer*, vol. 39 (May 1984), pp. 1094–95. Recently Bell and antitrust attorney Ira M. Millstein asked the Senate Judiciary Committee to consider legislation that would make price-fixing defendants liable only for the amount of damages they caused, based on their market share. Under such a law, plaintiffs would no longer be permitted to threaten a single defendant with the possibility of paying all of the treble damages attributed to the members of a horizontal price-fixing conspiracy. The plan would thereby sharply limit a remaining defendant's responsibility for a settling party's liability. See W. John Moore, "Two Lawyers Put New Wine in Contribution Bottle," *Legal Times*, May 6, 1985, p. 2.

101. The *locus classicus* for the distinction between choosing rules at the constitutional and post-constitutional levels of choice is James M. Buchanan and Gordon Tullock, *The Calculus of Consent* (Ann Arbor, Mich.: University of Michigan Press, 1962).

102. A modified contribution rule, that of claim reduction, has been discussed by Polinsky and Shavell, "Contribution and Claim Reduction."

103. Risk aversion means that firm A prefers the large (even certain) probability of a small loss to a small probability of a large loss when the two losses are of equal actuarial value. The risk-preferring firm (firm P) gets more utility from the small probability of a large loss than from the larger possibility of a smaller loss, while the risk neutral firm (firm T) is indifferent between the two possibilities.

104. Point E might be interpreted as a compromise between full contribution and no contribution. For example, it could mean that contribution is limited to non-settling defendants so that a defendant who settled would be exempt from being sued for contribution; or it could be a point where liability for damages is reduced by the amount that the settling defendants would have been required to pay in contribution if no one had settled. The first consideration would affect the probability of paying damages, while the second would affect the potential damages to be paid.

105. Breit and Elzinga, "Antitrust Penalties and Attitudes Toward Risk," pp. 704–06, and the studies cited therein.

106. This point has been stressed by Easterbrook, Landes, and Posner, "Contribution among Defendants," p. 352.

107. See Steven Shavell, "Risk Sharing and Incentives in the Principal and Agent Relationship," *Bell Journal of Economics*, vol. 10 (Spring 1979), pp. 55–73.

108. See Polinsky and Shavell, "Contribution and Claim Reduction," p. 452.

Polinsky and Shavell point out that strong indirect evidence of risk aversion in firms is the widespread purchase of property and liability insurance by corporations.

109. This is consistent with the results of Easterbrook, Landes, and Posner, "Contribution Among Defendants." The strong conclusion is disputed by Polinsky and Shavell on the grounds that corporate decision makers might themselves be insulated from corporate liability. If corporate managers are punished by salary reductions, diminished promotion prospects, or termination, much smaller sums are involved than the firm's trebled damages. In such a case it could be that the certainty of liability is a greater deterrent than the magnitude of that liability. If so, contribution would be a greater deterrent than no-contribution. However, this would not be the case if, as seems plausible, there were some threshold level of liability below which no internal sanctions would be imposed on decision makers. See Polinsky and Shavell, "Contribution and Claim Reduction," p. 455.

110. See, however, Dewey, "Information, Entry, and Welfare" and George Bittlingmayer, "Decreasing Average Cost and Competition: A New Look at the Addyston Pipe Case," *Journal of Law & Economics*, vol. 25 (October 1982), pp. 201–29.

111. The taxonomy draws on our discussion in "Antitrust Enforcement and Economic Efficiency," pp. 335–45.

112. Mark V. Pauly, "The Economics of Moral Hazard: Comment," *American Economic Review*, vol. 58 (June 1968), pp. 531–37.

113. See Woodner Theaters Inc. v. Paramount Pictures Corp., 333 F. Supp. 658 (E. D. La. 1970). For other illustrations, see Breit and Elzinga, "Antitrust Enforcement and Economic Efficiency," pp. 335–38.

114. Henry N. Butler, "Restricted Distribution Contracts and the Opportunistic Pursuit of Treble Damages," *Washington University Law Quarterly*, vol. 59 (December 1983), pp. 27–60. In a related context, Posner earlier had recognized, "Once a dealer is identified as a chronic discounter, he may even be able to violate lawful provisions of the dealership agreement with impunity, because the enforcement of *any* provisions against it may be deemed to have been motivated by its discounting." Richard A. Posner, "The Next Step in the Antitrust Treatment of Restricted Distribution Practices: Per Se Legality," *University of Chicago Law Review*, vol. 48 (Winter 1981), pp. 6–26 at p. 12.

115. "Private Brands and Antitrust Policy," *UCLA Law Review*, vol. 25 (October 1977), pp. 46–69.

116. Ibid., p. 62.

117. Compare State Wholesale Grocers v. Great Atlantic & Pacific Tea Co., 202 F. Supp. 768, 777 (N.D. Ill. 1961), with Lehrman v. Gulf Oil Corp., 464 F.2d 26, 46 (5th Cir. 1972) and Lehrman v. Gulf Oil Corp., 500 F.2d 659, 666 (5th Cir. 1974).

118. SCM Corp. v. Xerox Corp., 463 F. Supp. 983, 990 (Conn. 1978). But in holding for Xerox, the court of appeals did "seriously question the appropriateness of applying the avoidable consequences doctrine to a case such as this one," but chose not to resolve the issue since it held against SCM on

other grounds. SCM Corp. v. Corp., 645 F.2d 1195, 1208 n.8 (2nd Cir. 1981).

119. "Maternity Shop's Claims Against Maker of Strollers Are Doomed By Lack of Evidence," *BNA Antitrust & Trade Regulation Report*, vol. 47 (July 5, 1984), pp. 12–13.

120. 555 F.2d 426 (5th Cir. 1977).

121. Ibid., p. 436.

122. See H. Laurence Ross, *Settled Out of Court: The Social Process of Insurance Claims Adjustment* (Chicago: Aldine Publishing Co., 1970), pp. 204–11.

123. "Divorcement, Below-Cost Bill Would Interfere with Competitive Process," *BNA Antitrust & Trade Regulation Report*, vol. 48 (May 23, 1985), p. 891.

124. Arthur D. Austin, "Negative Effects of Treble Damage Actions: Reflections on the New Antitrust Strategy," *Duke Law Journal*, vol. 1978 (January 1978), pp. 1353–74.

125. Ibid.

126. See "Trustbusting: A New Role for Companies," *Business Week*, August 12, 1972, pp. 51–54.

127. Austin, "Negative Effects," pp. 1356–62.

128. Berkey Photo Inc. v. Eastman Kodak Co., 457 F. Supp. 404 (SDNY 1978), reversed, 603 F.2d 263 (2d Cir. 1979).

129. Austin, "Negative Effects," p. 1365, quoting Gerald Brock, *The U.S. Computer Industry* (Cambridge, Mass.: Ballinger Publishing Co., 1975), p. 172, note 79.

130. As reported in Malcolm E. Wheeler, "Antitrust Treble-Damage Actions: Do They Work?" *California Law Review*, vol. 61 (December 1973), pp. 1319–52 at p. 1325.

131. Ibid., p. 1339.

132. Robert B. Reich, "The Antitrust Industry," *Georgetown Law Journal*, vol. 68 (June 1980), pp. 1053–73 at pp. 1068–70. The figure is for the year 1979.

133. Wheeler, "Antitrust Treble-Damage Actions," p. 1349. The idea (as Wheeler gives credit) goes back to Richard A. Posner, "Oligopoly and the Antitrust Laws: A Suggested Approach," *Stanford Law Review*, vol. 21 (June 1969), pp. 1562–1606 at pp. 1590–92.

134. 15 U.S.C. 4001–21 (1982).

135. See Antitrust Reciprocity Act of 1982, 15 U.S.C. 15 (1982).

136. Pfizer, Inc. v. Government of India, 434 U.S. 308 (1978).

137. Local Government Antitrust Act of 1984, 15 U.S.C.A. §§ 34–36 (Supp. 1985).

138. 15 U.S.C.A. §§ 4301–05 (Supp. 1985).

139. U.S. Congress, House of Representatives, Subcommittee on Investigations and Oversight and the Subcommittee on Science, Research and Technology of the House Committee on Science and Technology, *Japanese Technological Advances and Possible United States Responses Using Research Joint Ventures: Hearings before the Subcommittee on Investigations and Oversight and the Subcommittee on Science, Research and Technology of the House Committee on Science and Technology*, 98th Congress, 1st session, 1983, p. 159. (Statement of William F. Baxter, then Assistant Attorney General, Antitrust Division).

140. Baxter, House of Representatives, Committee on Science and Technology, *Japanese Technological Advances*, p. 160.

141. "National Innovation and Productivity Act of 1983, 301 (c)," reprinted in *BNA Antitrust & Trade Regulation Report*, vol. 44 (June 30, 1983), pp. 1272–73.

142. To quote the testimony of then head of the Antitrust Division, William F. Baxter: ". . . the threat of mandatory treble damages is a necessary and appropriate deterrent to conduct that is clearly anticompetitive and carried out in secret, as in the case of price fixing among competitors. Such a punitive damage remedy is counterproductive, however, when it applies to conduct that can be procompetitive and is carried out in the open. Because treble damages greatly increase the cost associated with the risk that some court might incorrectly condemn a particular procompetitive practice, the remedy can inhibit a wide variety of procompetitive arrangements." Baxter, House of Representatives, Committee on Science and Technology, *Japanese Technological Advances*, p. 160.

143. Posner, *Antitrust Law*, p. 231. "The provision of treble damages in such cases serves simply to draw excessive enforcement resources into attempts to discover and prosecute such violations and to expand the prohibitions of the law. Only single damages should be allowed in such cases." p. 227.

144. Blair, "Antitrust Penalties," p. 70.

145. During a time of inflation, the rate of interest not only may compensate lenders for the time value of their money but may also reflect the fact that dollars paid back in the future have less real purchasing power. Plaintiffs who receive damages in indexed dollars would be fully compensated against the effects of inflation. The real rate of interest, which is the nominal (or money) interest rate less the rate of inflation, must be used to compensate them for the time value of the money they lost because of antitrust injury.

146. Areeda and Turner, *Antitrust Law*, p. 151.

147. Richard B. McKenzie, ed., *A Blueprint for Jobs and Industrial Growth* (Washington, D.C.: Heritage Foundation, 1983), pp. 23–24.

148. Committee for Economic Development, Subcommittee on Industrial Strategy and Trade, *Strategy for U.S. Industrial Competitiveness* (New York, 1984), pp. 112–13.

149. Mary Ella McBrearty, "Antitrust Treatment of Competitive Torts: An Argument for a Rule of Per Se Legality under the Sherman Act," *Texas Law Review*, vol. 58 (February 1980), pp. 415–34 at p. 415. McBrearty argues that "the Act's misapplication to these competitive torts actually may result in decreased competition and thereby vitiate the central purpose of antitrust law."

150. Posner, "The Chicago School of Antitrust Analysis," pp. 925–48.

151. Posner, *Antitrust Law*, pp. 227–28.

152. Areeda and Turner, *Antitrust Law*, p. 150.

153. Ibid., p. 35.

154. Ibid., p. 36.

155. "Notwithstanding the increasing volume of private antitrust suits,

government-initiated actions are the key to enforcement of the antitrust laws. They are undertaken in the public interest, addressed to more significant restraints and backed by substantial resources." Ibid., p. 131.

156. Robert H. Bork, *The Antitrust Paradox* (New York: Basic Books, 1978), pp. 406–07.

157. Elzinga and Breit, *The Antitrust Penalties*, pp. 3–14.

158. Ibid. For a description of the difficulties in privatizing antitrust, see Warren F. Schwartz, "An Overview of the Economics of Antitrust Enforcement," *Georgetown Law Review*, vol. 68 (June 1980), pp. 1075–1102, especially 1091–1100. See also, A. Mitchell Polinsky, "Private Versus Public Enforcement of Fines," *Journal of Legal Studies*, vol. 9 (1980), p. 105.

159. Elzinga and Breit, *Antitrust Penalties*, pp. 134–37 and pp. 150–51. The proposed fine would be 25 percent of the firm's pre-tax profits for every year of anticompetitive activity.

160. "Our empirical results suggest that, contrary to conventional wisdom, it is severity and not certainty that is most important in controlling bid-rigging. . . . The apparently unanticipated shift in penalties for bid-rigging that began in the late 1970's appears to have had a profound effect on the willingness of contractors to rig bids." Block, Feinstein, and Nold, "The Effectiveness of Recent U.S. Government Criminal Antitrust Enforcement Efforts," pp. 34, 38. The authors' conclusions that it is the size of the penalty that deters and not the certainty of conviction are not contrary to the conventional wisdom of the new learning; the findings are precisely what would be expected in a world of risk-averse managers.

161. Roderick G. Dorman, "The Case for Compensation: Why Compensatory Components are Required for Efficient Antitrust Enforcement," *Georgetown Law Journal*, vol. 68 (June 1980), pp. 1113–20 at 1118–19. "Without the promise of compensation to the injured party, the private attorney cannot effectively predispose the jury to his position. In enforcement systems not based on compensation, the attorney does not have the benefit of the dynamic from which actual damage awards result."

162. Irwin M. Stelzer, Procedures for Private Antitrust Enforcement in the United States, Second Oxford International Anti-Trust Law Conference, pp. 6–7, September 12, 1983, mimeo, citing Statistical Analysis of Private Antitrust Litigation: Final Report, October 30, 1979.

163. Austin, "Negative Effects of Treble Damage Actions," pp. 1372–73.

164. Kenneth W. Dam, "Class Actions: Efficiency, Compensation, Deterrence, and Conflict of Interest," *Journal of Legal Studies*, vol. 4 (January 1975), pp. 47–73 at pp. 67–69. "Private enforcement has relatively little to commend itself if it merely involves collection of treble damages after public enforcement agencies have established the violation. Then private enforcement only substitutes for an adequate system of public penalties." Ibid., p. 68.

165. Warren F. Schwartz, *Private Enforcement of the Antitrust Laws* (Washington, D.C.: American Enterprise Institute for Public Policy Research, 1981), pp. 26–27.

166. A. D. Neale and D. G. Goyder, *The Antitrust Laws of the United States of America* (New York: Cambridge University Press, 1981), pp. 26–27.

167. Note, "Controlling Jury Damage Awards in Private Antitrust Suits," *University of Michigan Law Review*, vol. 81 (January 1983), pp. 693–713 at pp. 694–96.

168. Ibid., p. 697 and the sources cited therein.

169. In the worst of all worlds for a defendant, a jury mistakenly believes *it* is to treble the damage estimate, does so, and reports this amount to the court, which the court then trebles.

170. "IBM Is Granted Directed Verdict In Memorex Case," *Wall Street Journal*, August 14, 1978, p. 3.

171. A federal judge in one of the IBM antitrust trials said that "the magnitude and complexity of the case . . . render it as a whole beyond the competency of any jury to understand and decide rationally." As quoted in Richard A. Shaffer, "Those Complex Antitrust Cases," *Wall Street Journal*, August 29, 1978, p. 16. William Baxter has indicated, "All but the simplest antitrust cases these days are totally beyond the comprehension of any jury you're likely to get." Ibid. See also, "Burger Sees Complex Trials Beyond Capacity of Jurors," *Washington Post*, August 8, 1979, p. A4.

172. Elzinga and Breit, *The Antitrust Penalties*, pp. 30–43.

173. Bane, *The Electrical Equipment Conspiracies: The Treble Damage Action*.

174. James M. Clabault and John F. Burton, Jr., *Sherman Act Indictments 1955–1965: A Legal and Economic Analysis* (New York: Federal Legal Publications, 1966), p. 45.

175. Elzinga and Breit, *The Antitrust Penalties*, pp. 32–33.

176. 15 U.S.C. §§ 1–3 (1976).

177. Joseph C. Gallo, Joseph L. Craycraft, and Steven C. Bush, "Guess Who Came to Dinner: An Empirical Study of Federal Antitrust Enforcement for the Period 1953–1984," *Review of Industrial Organization*, vol. II, no. 2 (1985), forthcoming.

178. Elzinga and Breit, *The Antitrust Penalties*, p. 33.

179. Gallo, Craycraft, and Bush, "Guess Who Came to Dinner."

180. Becker, "Crime and Punishment," pp. 179–80.

181. As quoted in Elzinga and Breit, *The Antitrust Penalties*, p. 42.

182. "McGrath's Maiden Speech Focuses on Criminal Enforcement," *BNA Antitrust & Trade Regulation Report*, vol. 46 (February 2, 1984), p. 179.

183. Richard A. Posner, "Optimal Sanctions for White-Collar Criminals," *American Criminal Law Review*, vol. 17 (1980), pp. 409–18.

184. Others have followed Becker and Posner in urging the greater efficiency of fines over imprisonment. See A. Mitchell Polinsky and Steven Shavell, "The Optimal Use of Fines and Imprisonment," *Journal of Public Economics*, vol. 24 (June 1984), pp. 89–99. (Arguing that it is desirable to use a fine to the maximum extent possible before supplementing it with an imprisonment term because imprisonment is socially costly relative to fines.) See also, Michael K. Block and Robert C. Lind, "Crime and Punishment Reconsidered," *Journal of Legal Studies*, vol. 4 (January 1975), pp. 241–47, and Block and Lind, "An Economic Analysis of Crimes Punishable by Imprisonment," *Journal of Legal Studies*, vol. 4 (June 1975), pp. 479–92. Although Block and Lind do not stress the optimal choice of sanctions, the premise of

their chief proposition (that in order to be certain an offender will pay whatever fine is levied he must be threatened with a prison sentence more severe than the fine) is that imprisonment is less efficient than fines as a method of punishment. For an opposing view see John Collins Coffee, Jr., "Corporate Crime and Punishment: A Non-Chicago View of the Economics of Criminal Sanctions," *American Criminal Law Review*, vol. 17 (1980), pp. 419–76.

185. Elzinga and Breit, *The Antitrust Penalties*, p. 56.

186. Gallo, Craycraft, and Bush, "Guess Who Came to Dinner."

187. Public Law 98-596, 98th Congress, October 30, 1984. 98 Stat. 3134.

188. "ABA Spring Meeting Examines Changes In Antitrust Enforcement," *BNA Antitrust & Trade Regulation Report*, vol. 48 (March 28, 1985), pp. 538–50 at p. 544.

189. Sims, ed., "New Approaches to Antitrust Damages," p. 1094, transcript of remarks of Jonathan C. Rose.

SELECTED AEI PUBLICATIONS

Essays in Contemporary Economic Problems: The Impact of the Reagan Program, Phillip Cagan, ed. (1986, approx. 370 pp., cloth $20.95, paper $10.95)

The Politics of Industrial Policy, Claude E. Barfield and William A. Schambra, eds. (1986, 344 pp., cloth $20.95, paper $10.95)

Crisis in the Budget Process: Exercising Political Choice, Allen Schick, with papers by David Stockman, Rudolph Penner, Trent Lott, Leon Panetta, and Norman Ornstein (1986, 88 pp., $4.95)

Protectionism: Trade Policy in Democratic Societies, Jan Tumlir (1985, 72 pp., $4.95)

Futures Markets: Their Economic Role, Anne E. Peck, ed. (1985, 325 pp., $21.95)

Futures Markets: Regulatory Issues, Anne E. Peck, ed. (1985, 376 pp., $24.95)

Real Tax Reform: Replacing the Income Tax, John H. Makin (1985, 42 pp., $3.95)

U.S. Agricultural Policy: The 1985 Farm Legislation, Bruce L. Gardner, ed. (1985, 385 pp., cloth $22.95, paper $12.95)

• *Mail orders for publications to:* AMERICAN ENTERPRISE INSTITUTE, 1150 Seventeenth Street, N.W., Washington, D.C. 20036 • *For postage and handling, add 10 percent of total; minimum charge $2, maximum $10 (no charge on prepaid orders)* • *For information on orders, or to expedite service, call toll free 800-424-2873 (in Washington, D.C., 202-862-5869)* • *Prices subject to change without notice.* • *Payable in U.S. currency through U.S. banks only*

AEI ASSOCIATES PROGRAM

The American Enterprise Institute invites your participation in the competition of ideas through its AEI Associates Program. This program has two objectives: (1) to extend public familiarity with contemporary issues; and (2) to increase research on these issues and disseminate the results to policy makers, the academic community, journalists, and others who help shape public policies. The areas studied by AEI include Economic Policy, Education Policy, Energy Policy, Fiscal Policy, Government Regulation, Health Policy, International Programs, Legal Policy, National Defense Studies, Political and Social Processes, and Religion, Philosophy, and Public Policy. For the $49 annual fee, Associates receive

- a subscription to *Memorandum,* the newsletter on all AEI activities
- the AEI publications catalog and all supplements
- a 30 percent discount on all AEI books
- a 40 percent discount for certain seminars on key issues
- subscriptions to any two of the following publications: *Public Opinion,* a bimonthly magazine exploring trends and implications of public opinion on social and public policy questions; *Regulation,* a bimonthly journal examining all aspects of government regulation of society; and *AEI Economist,* a monthly newsletter analyzing current economic issues and evaluating future trends (or for all three publications, send an additional $12).

Call 202/862-7170 or write: AMERICAN ENTERPRISE INSTITUTE
1150 Seventeenth Street, N.W., Suite 301, Washington, D.C. 20036